the Faithful

Heroes of the Old Testament

PRISCILLA SHIRER
KELLY MINTER
BETH MOORE
JENNIFER ROTHSCHILD
LISA HARPER

LifeWay Press® | Nashville, Tennessee

ISBN: 978-1-5359-3354-4
Item: 005809760

Dewey Decimal Classification: 221.92
Subject Headings: BIBLE. O.T.--BIOGRAPHY / FAITH / CHRISTIAN LIFE

To order additional copies of this resource, order online at www.lifeway.com; write LifeWay Christian Resources Customer Service: One LifeWay Plaza, Nashville, TN 37234; fax order to 615.251.5933; or call toll-free 1.800.458.2772.
Printed in the United States of America

Adult Ministry Publishing,LifeWay Resources, One LifeWay Plaza,Nashville, TN 37234

Cover by Alexis Ward of The Visual Republic

PRODUCTION TEAM

Director, LifeWay
Adult Ministry:
Faith Whatley

Editorial Manager:
Michelle Hicks

Content Editor:
Elizabeth Hyndman

Art Director:
Heather Wetherington

Editorial Intern:
Amanda Smith

Video Producer:
Lisa Turner

Video Director:
Bill Cox

TABLE OF CONTENTS

ABOUT THIS STUDY

THIS BIBLE STUDY IS UNIQUE.

- Each session comes from a previously published LifeWay Bible study.

- Each session was written by a different author.

- Each session has video teaching, but the videos vary in length.

- Each author brings her particular style and pacing to the video teaching and personal study.

BECAUSE THIS STUDY IS UNIQUE, YOU CAN USE IT DIFFERENT WAYS.

- Conduct the study as a regular consecutive-week study.

- Use this study as a retreat curriculum.

- Use a session or two to fill the gap between other Bible studies.

- Complete the study personally, with your leadership team, or full group to preview the five studies and authors represented.

REGARDLESS OF HOW YOU CHOOSE TO STUDY, WE RECOMMEND YOU CHECK OUT THE LEADER GUIDE.

Located on page 159, the leader guide offers several tips and helps along with discussion guides for each week. If you are leading a group, look over it ahead of time to prepare. We hope you'll find it helpful!

INTRODUCTION

Hebrews 11 begins,

> Now faith is the reality of what is hoped for, the proof of what is not seen. For by it our ancestors won God's approval. (vv. 1-2)

The next thirty-eight verses tell of the faithfulness of our ancestors in the faith— how they lived in the reality of what is hoped for, even when they couldn't see it. They trusted in God, the true faithful One, to fulfill His promises to them. They acted as if there were never any doubt He would do so.

Thousands of years after the men and women of the Old Testament walked the earth, we still can learn from their examples. We can learn to live in the reality of what is hoped for. We can learn to trust in the One who is faithful.

As we study the lives of four men and one woman who demonstrated obedience and trust in the steadfastness of our God, we hope you are encouraged. God fulfills His promises—every last one. He is worthy of our faith, our trust, and our hope.

Following what is often called the "Hall of Faith" in Hebrews 11, the next chapter begins with the answer to our "now what" question.

> Therefore, since we also have such a large cloud of witnesses surrounding us, let us lay aside every hindrance and the sin that so easily ensnares us. Let us run with endurance the race that lies before us, keeping our eyes on Jesus, the source and perfecter of our faith. For the joy that lay before him, he endured the cross, despising the shame, and sat down at the right hand of the throne of God.
> **HEBREWS 12:1-2**

These men and women—the faithful ones—surround us. Their stories shout the truth about our God. He is good, He is sovereign, He is wise, He is faithful.

Our God has been with His people through war, exile, persecution, uncertainty, and silence. He is still with us today. That is what the faithful shout to us as we run. He is with you.

With these testimonies in our hearts and minds, we can run the race set before us with endurance. They surround us, but Jesus is ahead. We keep our eyes on Jesus—both the beginning and the completion of our faith.

For every one of God's promises is "Yes" in him.
2 CORINTHIANS 1:20a

These Old Testament heroes of the faith all point to Him—the One sitting at the right hand of the throne of God, the One who is the fulfillment of every promise.

God's providence will never take us to a place where God's grace can't sustain us.

Gideon

Our first hero lived during the time of the judges. Often described as timid, reserved, and questioning, Gideon made an unlikely hero. Despite his fear, Gideon stayed faithful to his calling.

The period of the Israelite judges lay between the conquest of the promised land under Joshua and the rise of the monarchy with Saul and David. The events described in the Book of Judges took place from the early fourteenth century B.C. to the latter part of the eleventh century B.C., a period of around three hundred fifty years. This was a time of social and religious anarchy, characterized by the repeated refrain, "In those days there was no king in Israel; everyone did whatever seemed right to him" (Judg. 17:6).

In the midst of this chaos, God called timid Gideon to lead His people.

As the fifth judge of Israel, Gideon's primary purpose was to relieve military pressure on the tribes of Israel and deliver them from the oppression of foreign nations.

The judges God appointed were different from our judges today. They were men and women called by God and empowered by God to unite the people of God to stand against the enemies of God.

God handpicked terribly flawed people to be judges, and then empowered them to fulfill the role in spite of their shortcomings. He chose people from circles that seemed inappropriate to observers.

Likewise, God used scared, questioning Gideon to lead as a "valiant warrior" (Judg. 6:12).

Gideon's story challenges and encourages us to live out our callings in the midst of fear. It shows us God can take fearful people and make them into valiant warriors by His power.

We'll see God's sovereignty in the life of Gideon. We'll see God is the One who gives us both identity and purpose. We'll learn what it's like to be faithful in the midst of crisis. And we'll learn, in the words of Lisa Harper, "Our weakness nor a national crisis can circumvent God's sovereignty."

ABOUT GIDEON: YOUR WEAKNESS. GOD'S STRENGTH.

Originally published in 2013, *Gideon: Your Weakness. God's Strength.* is a 7-session women's Bible study by Priscilla Shirer. This study will encourage you to recognize your weakness as the key that the Lord gives you to unlock the full experience of His strength in your life.

ABOUT PRISCILLA

Through the expository teaching of the Word of God, Priscilla desires to see people not only know the uncompromising truths of Scripture intellectually but experience them practically by the power of the Holy Spirit.

For the past twenty years, Priscilla has been in full-time ministry to women. She and her husband, Jerry, founded Going Beyond Ministries and count it as their privilege to serve believers across the entire spectrum of the body of Christ. Priscilla is the author of more than a dozen books and Bible studies on a myriad of topics and biblical people including *Discerning the Voice of God*, *The Armor of God*, *Fervent*, and *Gideon*.

WEEK

1

WHAT TO EXPECT WHEN YOU'RE EXPECTING

Then the angel of the LORD came and sat under the oak that was in Ophrah, which belonged to Joash the Abiezrite as his son Gideon was beating out wheat in the wine press in order to save it from the Midianites. The angel of the LORD appeared to him and said: "The LORD is with you, valiant warrior."

JUDGES 6:11-12

Are we/Am I being faithful in the mundane/small thi...
Luke 19:17

omnipresence - manifest presence -
seen by God
known, forgiven, called, empowered

DISTINGUISHING CHARACTERISTICS OF THE MIDIANITES:

You know you are dealing with the Midianites when the trouble is coming from the most ___unexpected___ place.

You know you are dealing with the Midianites because just when you get your ___head___ above ___water___, that problem ___resurfaces___ again.

WHAT SHOULD YOU EXPECT WHEN YOU'RE EXPECTING?

1. The crisis is not ___powerful___ enough to place you out of the ___reach___ of God.
Isaiah 59:1

2. The [crisis] does ___position___ you for your ___calling___.
Judges 6:12-13 *(11-14)*

God is more interested in changing your ___heart___ than He is your ___circumstances___
Luke 19:17

God had a message for Gideon.
individual vs collective

Legacy -
don't know
whom going
through it

Hebrews 11:32-34

Judges 6:12

Gideon was faithful to the task even
though inconvenient/difficult

No matter how you feel, what the ___Scripture___ says about you is ___true___.
1 Peter 2:9

Progression:
came
appeared
Lord looked

3. Your crisis does not ___dictate___ your ___capability___
Judges 6:11-12, 14

even if we
don't know it

The angel of the LORD ___came___ (v. 11), ___appeared___ (v. 12), ___looked___ (v. 14).

Always calling out of your chaos. Always go back to Word.

12   THE FAITHFUL   *Feelings don't have intellect*
Warrior princess / daughter of the King

Always look upward & outward — not inward
What God says about us is what's true

expected devastation from the Midianites - repeated
    eighth invasion during Gideon's time

Midianites came from Abraham also → unexpected
Israelites had done all the hard work ...

Gideon marked by insecurity & timidity & fear
hid himself and his harvest → to be unnoticed
Angel of Lord - theophany - preincarnation of Christ
God found him
Cannot outrun hound of heaven. His arm is long.

Dorrie
Don't cry for me because God met me there

Gideon tried to thresh wheat in winepress -
the opposite environment - yet where God called him.
    also difficult & inconvenient - faithful
God uses all things for our good and His glory.

Word written ON our hearts, not in it
Heart breaks and Word fell into our hearts.
Everything is God ordained or God allowed.
        arranged
            He will use it.

COMMISSIONING GIDEON

Yesterday, I walked into my bedroom to grab a book from my bedside table. Sliding past a chair in the corner, I scoured the table for the book. As I turned to leave, I nearly jumped out of my socks when an enormous shadowy figure suddenly moved in the corner.

My husband, all two hundred fifty pounds of him, had been sitting in that corner chair the whole time, watching me search. He had seen me, but I hadn't seen him. Not until he started to get up did I even realize he was there.

We have come upon one of the most fascinating parts of the entire narrative of Gideon's story: Gideon's encounter with the angel of the LORD.

> Then the angel of the LORD came and sat under the oak that was in Ophrah, which belonged to Joash the Abiezrite as his son Gideon was beating out wheat in the wine press in order to save it from the Midianites. The angel of the LORD appeared to him.
> **JUDGES 6:11-12, NASB**

Underline the three action verbs connected with "the angel of the LORD" in the passage above.

I wonder what caused Gideon to become aware of the angel's presence?

The angel of the LORD (Malak Yahweh) is described by scholar John Marshal Lang as the "Great presence in Israelite History." He was the eternal, pre-existent Christ, and His appearance was one of the astounding theophanies (God-appearances) in the Old Testament. Other appearances of the Malak Yahweh in the Old Testament: Genesis 16:7-13, Exodus 3:2, Numbers 22:22

Did the angel rise from his seated position? Did he make a quick movement that caught Gideon's eye? Did he cough or sniffle, maybe even clear his throat in a slightly sarcastic way?

The Hebrew word translated *appeared* in verse 12 suggests the angel presented himself, making himself visible to Gideon. The angel's actions made it possible for Gideon to see him. Scripture isn't clear as to what brought the angel to Gideon's attention, but the sequence of events is evident. In verse 11, the angel was sitting under the oak tree but not until verse 12 does it say he "appeared" to Gideon.

Whether he had been sitting there for only a few seconds or perhaps for several minutes (or longer) is unclear. But what we can deduce from the text is this: the angel finding Gideon was a separate occurrence from Gideon finding the angel.

This means that probably no lightning strike accompanied the angel's arrival. Nor was he sparkling in a shimmering haze. He wasn't a see-through, floating immortal who hovered inches above the ground, and no flash mob broke into the "Hallelujah Chorus" to herald his arrival. No, this angel most likely had the look of an ordinary man who had come to Gideon in an ordinary way during an ordinary day.

God often comes to us in our "boring" days, veiled in the most ordinary of circumstances. In fact, "ordinary" is often the disguise of the divine. If we are constantly anticipating a grandiose event to accompany the times when we encounter Him or hear His voice, we will miss out on many intimate moments in our relationship with God. The mundane, the routine, the commonplace—these are often the contexts in which He will reveal Himself to humanity.

Having your spiritual radar up in consistent anticipation of His presence—even in the midst of the joyful chaos and regular rhythms of your everyday living—is paramount in hearing God, because sometimes the place and manner you find Him is the least spectacular you'd expect.

Oh, yes, sometimes His presence has made the hair on the back of my neck stand straight up. But more often than not, flashy and flamboyant are not His style. Being mindful of this and recognizing Him even when His glory is shrouded in normalcy is a prerequisite for gaining clarity in your calling. To be aware of God's purpose, you must first be aware of His presence.

What expectations do you think believers have of how God reveals Himself?

How do you think these expectations have been formed?

Stories

How might these beliefs keep people from recognizing a God encounter in their lives?

thinking error

SEEING GOD

In Ephesians 1:18-19, Paul records one amazingly long and spiritually rich sentence: "I pray that the eyes of your heart may be enlightened, so that you will know what is the hope of His calling, what are the riches of the glory of His inheritance in the saints, and what is the surpassing greatness of His power toward us who believe" (NASB).

Fill in the blanks to chart the progression in the verse.
Paul prays that the ___*eyes*___ of their hearts may be ___*enlightened*___. The result will be that they will ___*know*___ what is the ___*hope*___ of His ___*calling*___, the ___*riches*___ of the glory of His ___*inheritance*___, and the surpassing greatness of His ___*power*___ for believers.

Now that you've filled in the blanks above, go back and read the statement aloud. Take it in slowly and note the progression from one stage to the next. What summary idea do you take from the text?

see, know
hope, calling, promises, power

Do you see hints of these phases even in Gideon's case? He became aware of God's presence first and then discovered a new calling and the power to accomplish it. The same pattern is true for us. As believers, our spiritual eyes must detect God's presence. Once this happens, the opportunity unfolds for us to understand our calling and the vast inheritance we've been given to accomplish the tasks before us.

We often want to get on with the purposes of God (especially if we think doing so will get us out from under the shadow of the oak tree), forgoing the necessary prefix to that reality—becoming aware of and honoring His presence with us. First the angel caused Gideon to become aware of his nearness, then he spoke God's Word to him.

Consider Samuel's example. Read 1 Samuel 3:4-11. Then number each statement in chronological order.

4   Samuel is entrusted with a message from God.

3   Samuel says, "Speak, LORD, for Your servant is listening."

1   God speaks but Samuel is unaware that it is God.

2   Samuel's mentor helps him realize that God is speaking.

Apparently, God's voice was unaccompanied by pomp and fanfare. In fact, it was so unexciting that it sounded like the voice of an aged man. Had God not persisted, Samuel might not have ever realized that this ordinary voice belonged to an extraordinary Being.

I wonder how often God has been near, but I haven't noticed because I assumed that His nearness would always be coupled with astonishing circumstances.

Today, Gideon's story encourages us to seek the Almighty in the midst of normalcy. Ask the Lord to make Himself visible to you just as He did to Gideon. Pray that He will open your spiritual eyes over the next twenty-four hours so you can see Him more clearly than ever before.

TODAY I LEARNED:

God is faithful.
My calling includes small things.
He can and will help me if I will
   watch and receive it.
I need to look for God's power in His
   Word, His world, and believe it
   is in me.
Open the eyes of my heart, Lord.

THRESHING AND OTHER ORDINARY THINGS

The plumbers are here today. They've determined the house needs a complete plumbing renovation. The pipes are old, rusted, and leaking everywhere. Everything needs replacing. All of it.

Our plumber is a kind man who has delivered the news as gently as possible. The expense of overhauling the whole system is staggering. Perhaps it was the whites of our eyes or the shortness of our breath that caused him to make the offer, but right after he told us the repair price, he threw in a few extras for free—a couple of new toilets and a new tankless water heater. His reasoning: "All my work is going to be underground. It's always nice to see something happening above the ground too."

He's right. Seeing something change always helps. In fact, if we look at what Gideon was doing when his angelic visitor appeared, we'll see the above-ground evidence of things happening below the surface in his life.

So today we have a lesson in threshing.

Write anything you know about the purpose and process of threshing.

purification/sorting/cleaning

THRESHING

At this point in the year in Gideon's story, wise farmers could be found threshing—separating the meaty, nutrient-rich grain from the light, airy, and useless chaff. Typically, the wheat harvest would be taken to an open-air station called a threshing floor, where oxen pulling a heavy slab would trample it underfoot. This process yielded a better result in less time than threshing the wheat by hand. Gideon had neither the luxury of taking his harvest to a threshing floor nor the desire to attract the Midianites' attention by doing his threshing in public.

For more study: Chaff was often used as imagery for spiritual principles.
Here are some examples:

Psalm 1:4 • Psalm 83:13 • Isaiah 33:11 • Luke 3:17

Instead, Gideon was working in a winepress—a small enclosed space—and most likely using a small instrument called a flail (two thick boards fused together, studded with sharp stone fragments on one side) to slowly knock the grain loose from the stalk. Normally only the poor used this method. Imagine Gideon hunched over his stack of wheat, dedicated to the arduous task of a farmhand. His task was as mundane and necessary for him as washing the dinner dishes might be for you.

List five ordinary tasks you perform on a daily basis.

1. taking care of the dog

2. getting dressed

3. choosing food to eat

4. laundry email

5. getting ready for bed

Think back to the main points in yesterday's lesson. The angel appeared to Gideon in an ordinary way. Yet equally significant is the fact that he appeared while Gideon was doing an ordinary task—threshing wheat.

So, look back to the first paragraph of this section on threshing and underline the word that describes the key purpose of threshing.

separating wheat from chaff

SEPARATION

Raised in an agrarian culture, Gideon had become so accustomed to the routine of threshing that its familiarity may have blinded him to the significance of what God was subtly showing him. Gideon's physical act of separating grain from chaff pointed to his future task.

Turn to Judges 6:25-26 and record the details of the first task that Gideon would be asked to undertake.

- take the second bull, 7 years old
- tear down altar to Baal & cut down Asherah pole
- build proper altar to Lord on top of that height
- using wood of Asherah pole, offer bull as burnt offering

From what was God asking Gideon to begin separating Israel?

worship of Baal
his father

Gideon was being prepared to separate one nation from another, one kingdom from another, God's people from God's enemies. He would even be called to do some very personal threshing—separating himself from his own allegiance to Baal. Separation was about to become a big part of what God was calling him to do.

I love how Scripture does this—building layer upon layer of meaning into these "routine" biblical events. Remember, this is God's story; not just Gideon's. Even in the mundane detail of this timid farmer's experience, God was grooming him for his calling and for the separating process He was about to initiate with His people. This was not just a man threshing wheat; it was God painting some above-ground imagery for Gideon (and us) to see.

If we'll look around, we might also find Him preparing us as He works through our daily lives. Today's tasks—even the most mundane of them—are often preparation for tomorrow's calling. They can carry clues to what He is leading us to learn and accomplish as we faithfully serve Him.

While it might seem comical to find spiritual principles in washing dishes or answering phones at your desk job, God is teaching you faithfulness, diligence, and integrity through every task.

> Take a minute to pray. Ask the Lord to reveal a specific spiritual lesson He might be teaching you through one of the tasks you listed at the beginning of today's lesson. Record them as He reveals them.

all opportunities
do it with joy

UNSEEN ABUNDANCE

Separation was not the only thing God was communicating to Gideon through threshing. Based on what we know of the Israelites' ordeal at the time, it's hard to picture them as being fruitful, abundant, and prosperous. But the ordinary task of threshing sheds an interesting light on an easily overlooked perspective.

> Look up the following passages. What connection do both make between God's faithfulness and threshing?

Leviticus 26:3-5 *follow my decrees; obey His commands ... → all the food you want & live in safety*

Joel 2:24 *threshing floors will be filled with grain; the vats will overflow c new wine ¡ oil*

These verses describe a full threshing floor, overrun with a harvest resulting from God's favor. Threshing, in an agrarian biblical world, was a sign of abundance. In other words, the mere fact that Gideon had wheat to thresh was a symbol of God's favor expressed to His people, despite the hardship and oppression they were facing.

Gideon's story reveals that even your most mundane duty has a twinkle of the favor of God. For if He removed His blessings completely from you—taking away your home, your family, your work, your possessions—the need for many of your daily tasks would disappear. Don't despise the very things that signify your seat under the umbrella of God's goodness each day.

> Look back at the list of routine tasks you wrote down earlier. Beside each, write down what they indicate about God's faithfulness and kindness to you.

Gideon threshed because God was kind. Had God chosen to withhold that kindness, Israel would not only have been displaced and browbeaten by the enemy but would also have starved to death from lack of crops. Did Gideon realize that his threshing was a sign of God's favor on him and his people? Probably not. Was he so concerned about the enemy or bored by his task that he didn't realize his actions showed that Yahweh had not abandoned them? Probably so.

What about you? What about me?

I bet our top five ordinary tasks look similar—if not in exact detail, at least in their level of seeming importance. Most of our days are filled with routine duties required for life to continue with any sort of sanity. But if we take the time to look closely, we might discover that God is using these normal activities to prepare us for future tasks, each duty pointing to His blessings in our lives.

> End today's lesson by asking the Lord to help you be thankful for those ordinary tasks, to not despise them, and to see how He might be using them to prepare you for the future.

TODAY I LEARNED:

to be faithful ; watch for God

THE PRINCIPLE OF ABUNDANCE AND OPPRESSION

As you consider Gideon's abundance of wheat, don't miss an important principle. God's people were oppressed by the Midianites. Their dismal plight was a direct consequence of their rebellion. Gideon's tribe, Manasseh, like many other tribes in the nation, had not taken full possession of their land. They fell into idolatry as they mingled with the Canaanites. God was obviously not pleased, yet He supplied His people's needs. The fact that He chose to bless them with wheat to thresh does not imply that He had truly blessed them as a people. They had wheat, but not peace. Grain but not goodwill.

Having an ample wheat supply, therefore, in the midst of this rancid environment tells us something theologically important: both oppression and abundance can coexist in the lives of God's people. God's loyalty does not equal God's approval. In 1 Chronicles 21, for example, David's sin had resulted in dire consequences for Israel. A tormenting plague swept through the land for three days, wiping out seventy thousand people. Yet in the midst of this tragedy, the Bible says a guy named Ornan "was threshing wheat" (v. 20). Divine discipline and consequence were running rampant across the hills and valleys of Israel, yet the people were still experiencing the great mercy of the Lord (v. 13). How

do we know? Because their threshing floors remained full.

The harvest that God routinely allowed Israel's farmers to retain was not a sign of God's approval; it was a sign of His loyalty. I wonder if Israel ever confused the two. I wonder if we ever confuse them.

Consider and internalize the Principle of Abundance and Oppression:

1. God is still faithful to us even when we are faithless.

2. God's faithfulness does not signify God's approval.

May we never equate His faithfulness to us in times of rebellion with His endorsement or tolerance of our choices. When we are unfaithful to God, He will not excuse or overlook our sin. But because we are His, He will still demonstrate His love and care by remaining faithful to His covenant with us and populating our lives with certain blessings. These gifts are not designed to lull us into spiritual apathy or lighten the weight of our offenses. He intends to woo us—graciously, kindly, lavishly— back into intimate fellowship with Himself.

OVERLOOKING THE OBVIOUS

Ordinary.

This week we're learning that the ordinary is often the disguise of the divine. God often comes to us in ways that are unassuming, steadying us as we become aware of His constant, active presence. But because we often lose sight of His glory under a pile of routine activities, we sometimes miss the stunning and powerful messages He comes to give.

From Judges 6:12, record the first part of the declaration the angel made to Gideon.

What might have caused Gideon to doubt this revelation?

The Lord was with him? Really? If there was one thing Gideon felt extremely certain of, it was that God had completely abandoned him and his people. How else could their circumstances have become this disastrous for this long?

According to Judges 6:13, what questions did Gideon ask the angel?

The fact that Gideon had these frank, bold questions is understandable. For the seventh year in a row, Israel had been sitting ducks for Midian's annual hunting trip. Gideon, like anyone else in this scenario, had some questions about how these things could occur if God was as near as this stranger was suggesting.

If you're facing a season of difficulty, write down the questions you've been asking God on the left side of this chart. We'll come back to these thoughts a little later today.

QUESTIONS FOR GOD	HIS ANSWERS

There's nothing wrong with a question unless you've already been given the answer.

GIDEON'S QUESTIONS, GOD'S ANSWERS

Jude, my four-year-old, often asks me the same question over and over again, sometimes within the span of a few minutes.

"Mommy? Mommy? Mommy? Mommy?"

"Can I? Can I? Can I? Can I?"

While continuous questions can be bothersome, the only time I get truly unnerved is when I've already answered them. Doesn't he know by now that my answer isn't going to change—that once I've made up my mind, there's no point in asking again?

Maybe one day he'll figure it out.

Maybe one day I will too.

> Read Judges 6:8-10 in your Bible. Which of the following does verse 10 pinpoint as the source of Israel's problems?
>
> ☐ Israel had served idols and disobeyed God.
> ☐ Israel had been abandoned by God.
> ☐ Israel was living in the wrong land.

> Go back to Gideon's questions you recorded on page 25. Circle the one that Judges 6:10 answers.

In the midst of Israel's long, tumultuous plight, God had sent a nameless prophet to them. This anonymous bearer of divine insight had given the answer as to why terrible things were happening. Instead of needing to search out new information with the angel in verse 13, Gideon needed only to recall what he had heard some time before in verse 10.

Just like my four-year-old.

Just like me.

Far too often, I spend time asking God about matters He has already explained. In His Word, He has listed His decisions. I should not expect Him to change His mind just because I keep bringing it up. No matter how fervent the prayer or how pious my kneeling position, I cannot get a different answer out of God.

No need to ask Him about some things. He's written down His response in eternal ink. I might as well stop asking and start reading.

WHY DO YOU ASK?

Instead of answering Gideon's litany of complaints, the angel responded,

"Go in this your strength and deliver Israel from the hand of Midian.
Have I not sent you?"
JUDGES 6:14, NASB

Huh? I asked you a question, buddy. Let's start with an answer for that! But no answer would come to Gideon, for the angel had already moved on to other things. New things. God had already made Himself clear on the previous ones. The revelation of God's nearness and His previously given Word to the people were all Gideon would need for doing what He was being called to do.

The Lord's command to go forward in his strength was a reference to the Spirit's strength with which Yahweh intended to clothe and empower Gideon.

Now, I believe God graciously allows us to come to Him with questions that stir our souls when life doesn't make sense. But, Sister, God's Word has already spoken on so many of the topics that you and I are constantly asking questions about. Whether regarding our spiritual destiny or our practical daily experiences, we sometimes need only recall what God has already said to get the answer we are so fervently seeking in prayer.

It is wise to seek God for direction as we apply spiritual principles to specific decisions in our lives. But sometimes—sometimes—prayer and fasting are unnecessary steps in knowing what God is saying. When we feel God is ignoring us, could it be that His perceived silence is intended to point us back to His Word? Take time to see what's already written in Scripture. If God said it then, He still means it now.

Choose two of these verses to look up. Record what they say is clearly God's will for people.

Micah 6:8 • 1 Thessalonians 4:3 • 1 Thessalonians 5:18
Ephesians 6:6 • Matthew 22:37-38

THAT'S THE TRUTH

Gideon somehow experienced a disconnect between what he'd heard before and what he was currently facing. Either he never really gave God credit for all those miracles of deliverance and conquest (as the prophet had reminded Israel in Judges 6:8-10), or he just didn't think God was around anymore and willing to do those same things for him. He heard, "The LORD is with you," but he didn't believe it.

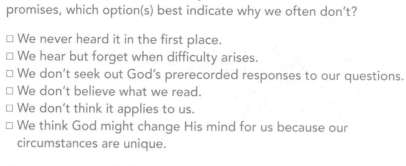

While we can't say for certain why Gideon failed to recall God's promises, which option(s) best indicate why we often don't?

☐ We never heard it in the first place.
☐ We hear but forget when difficulty arises.
☐ We don't seek out God's prerecorded responses to our questions.
☐ We don't believe what we read.
☐ We don't think it applies to us.
☐ We think God might change His mind for us because our circumstances are unique.

Choose one from the list that describes a frame of mind or attitude you've recently exhibited. What causes you to justify this response?

Consider our tendency to stress our own logic over God's truth. How do you see hints of this in today's portion of Gideon's story? How do we tend to react like Gideon did in this situation?

If you can't find biblical responses to your questions or uncertainties, take them to a spiritual leader who can help you find the answers in God's Word and pray with you about them.

No matter Gideon's reasons, you and I need to learn a lesson from this event: God's Word is sure, unchanging, and true. This means it doesn't vary or fall prey to our realities, no matter how difficult or even hopeful His statement is. Rather, His Word stands over our circumstances as the declarative reality to which all of our lives—and everything happening within them—must answer and be conformed.

The truth: Yahweh was with Gideon. The truth: He had been and still was their deliverer. The truth: Israel needed only to turn from her wickedness, and she would begin to see this fact clearly. God said it. Now Gideon needed to believe it and live according to it.

> Prayerfully consider answers God has already given to any of the questions you recorded earlier (page 25). Write your answers on the right side of the chart.

God is with you, Sister. Yeah, I'm talking to you. God is with you, just like He was with Gideon.

No matter what He's commissioning you to do—to fearlessly parent your children alone, faithfully submit to authority, courageously begin that ministry, boldly walk in moral purity, surrender to the demands of this season—whatever it is, recklessly follow Him. Because if He is with you, then no one and nothing can ever be against you.

TODAY I LEARNED:

WHO DO YOU THINK YOU ARE?

I looked in the mirror and grimaced at the sight of a dark spot on my lower back. I'd noticed it for the past two evenings while getting ready for bed, and I was officially concerned. I turned my back toward the mirror on my closet door and twisted my head around to take a good look.

What in the world could it be? I didn't know. But after watching it for two days, I knew one thing: I was calling the doctor in the morning.

I decided to mention it to my husband, who turned me around and took a quick peek. "Don't see anything," he said and returned to his book.

Unconvinced he was taking this seriously, I told him to look a second time … right … here. Again, he saw nothing. Either God had performed a quick miracle on me, or Jerry was in need of one—for blindness.

At that, I forced him into the bathroom with me, spun my body into the same position under the shaded bathroom lights, and pointed out the bruise I couldn't believe he couldn't see.

Thank goodness, he could finally spot it. He squinted his eyes into tiny slants two inches away from my skin. But after a few seconds, he grabbed my right elbow and tugged me six inches to the right, then smirked and walked back to the bedroom. The spot on my lower back was suddenly, amazingly, completely gone. It had been only a shadow.

A change in perspective changed everything.

SHIFTING SHADOWS

Gideon has had a shadow cast across his life. It has left him feeling deflated, worried, and dispirited. For seven years he has lived with an ominous Midianite silhouette settling itself across his soul, causing an outline of discouragement around him.

So one of the primary goals of the angel at the moment of their meeting was to give the soon-to-be judge a swift tug out of the shadows and into the clarifying light of Yahweh's perspective.

> Fill in the blanks from Judges 6:12 (HCSB):
>
> "The LORD is with you, _____ _____."
>
> Which of the following were the focus of this portion of the angel's message to Gideon?
> ☐ what he had been called to do
> ☐ whom he had been called to defeat
> ☐ who he was
> ☐ who was with him
> ☐ whom he had been called to lead

Mighty warrior in Hebrew is *gibbor chayil*, also translated as "mighty man of valor" in the King James Version. The terminology is the same used to describe David's valiant warriors who had executed courageous exploits on behalf of the king (1 Chron. 11:10-25). This label made sense for David's warriors. They were elite fighters, handpicked to perform special tasks. They were champions. When others wilted under pressure, these men stood their ground, undeterred in support of their new king.

> Underline the key words in the paragraph above that describe a *gibbor chayil*.
>
> Considering Gideon's current posture, what would have made the angel's statement ironic and unbelievable?

Gideon didn't have the look of a "mighty man of valor." Cowering silently in the winepress, Gideon felt and looked like anything other than valiant. Nobody would have described this man with our Hebrew term. But Yahweh's view was not bound by Gideon's reality or actions. Gideon may have been under the shadow of Midian, but Yahweh was not. He could see beyond the exterior, calling out of Gideon something that the timid man probably didn't even realize was in him. Gideon wasn't a scared farmer. Not really. That's how he was behaving, but that's not who he was.

Yahweh's perspective of us is often so unbelievable, so foreign to our own belief system and conduct that it can be like a bolt of lightning striking our desensitized souls. It jolts us away from the misplaced shadows of our experience into the truth of God's reality.

The angel had already told Gideon who was with him, but now he wanted to reveal what was in him. The angel knew that Gideon wouldn't respond well to the call until his perception of his potential was reformatted. So the angel tugged the would-be hero out of the shadows and into the clear, bright light of Yahweh's love.

Why do you think it is critical for believers to understand their identity before moving forward into their destiny?

If you've ever seen how an incorrect or malformed spiritual identity can hamper someone's spiritual success, describe it below.

BELIEVE IT OR NOT

So Gideon was a mighty warrior, huh? Well, apparently he wasn't buying it.

Read Gideon's response to the angel in Judges 6:13. How did Gideon deal with the angel's sentiments about him being a valiant warrior?
□ He refuted it.
□ He hesitantly acknowledged it.
□ He received it, believed it, and walked in it.
□ He ignored it completely.
□ He applied it to someone else.

Mark the pair of terms that best describe a disparity you've dealt with between your self-perception and a biblical view of who you are in Christ.

SELF-IMAGE	GOD-IMAGE	BIBLE REFERENCE
fearful	courageous	Josh. 1:9; Ps. 138:3
incompetent	capable	2 Cor. 3:5-6
ungifted	equipped	1 Cor. 1:4-8; Heb. 13:20-21
worthless	valuable	1 Pet. 2:9; Matt. 6:26
rejected	accepted	John 15:16
insignificant	special	Zeph. 3:17; Eph. 1:3-6

Have you seen this impact your ability to walk in a way that is pleasing to the Lord? If so, how?

Record the reasons why you chose the pair(s) of words you did, and then look up the corresponding verse(s) to read and prayerfully consider.

Keep a reminder of God's Word to you in this area of your life. On a 3x5 card, write the pair of words you selected. On the other side, record the Scripture God has given you for this issue. Keep it handy all week.

I cannot even begin to tell you how many times I've brushed past God's exclamations of His view of me. Sometimes, instead of acting in a way that is congruent with what He says, I casually dismiss it as something that might be true for others but not for me. Without Him, left to my own reality, I am all of those "fearful, incompetent, insignificant" things in the list. But with Him, my purposes and possibilities completely change.

Gideon was so skeptical of the description God had given him, he didn't even address the whole *gibbor chayil* title in his response. Immersed in the throes of devastation and disillusionment, he discussed another theme entirely. In essence, Gideon overlooked one of the most important portions of this heavenly interaction.

Sometimes, so do we.

Earlier, you selected the option that best describes how Gideon dealt with the angel's sentiments. Go back and circle the option that describes how you most often deal with what God says about you.

Think specifically about the passages you looked up earlier. Is there any part of God's viewpoint of your identity or potential that you have dismissed or disregarded? Why?

What would "receiving it, believing it, and walking in it" look like in your life? What would change about the next twenty-four hours of your life if you believed what God said?

GROUNDWORK

Sometimes we prematurely pursue the mission to which we've been called and forgo the critical groundwork of learning about and walking in our God-given spiritual identity. When life's shadows distort our reality, those distortions can easily become our truth, ripping us away from God's truth and thwarting our purpose.

The assignment for which God is calling us will go unrealized unless we are convinced of the spiritual chops He has given us to accomplish it. His perspective might sound unbelievable and even look completely incorrect based on the way we are acting and feeling. But trusting God and walking in His pronouncement of potential is the foundation of spiritual victory.

A believer without a clear sense of her true spiritual identity is like a police officer with no badge, like a driver with no license. They may have the right equipment, but they don't have the authority to use it.

Gideon was more than the sum of his cowardly parts. He was more than his circumstances. He was a valiant warrior touched by an encounter with God Himself. And you, my friend, are too.

Even if you are hiding in a winepress.

Even if you are running from an enemy.

Even if you are more humiliated now than ever before.

Even if intimidation and fear have been your constant companions.

Today, you're getting tugged out of the shadows. Now, lift up your head and act like it.

TODAY I LEARNED:

DAY 5

GIDEON'S ASSIGNMENT

"First things first." It's an adage quickly spouted and often as quickly ignored, because we don't know what we should prioritize or we don't like what's first in line when we do.

Any doubts that Gideon's visitor was heavenly had vanished from his mind right along with the angel from his sight (Judg. 6:21). He now knew for sure whom he'd been dealing with at his homemade threshing floor. So Gideon, his uncertainties quelled, built an altar (Judg. 6:24), signifying the beginning of his transfer of allegiance away from the false gods of his people.

As this change was beginning to burn hot in Gideon's heart and mind, Yahweh began to spell out Gideon's very first assignment. He was sending him to a mission field a lot closer than Gideon might have suspected.

Fill in the blanks from Judges 6:25:

Now on the same night the LORD said to him, "Take your father's young bull and a second bull seven years old, and _____ _____ the altar of _____ which belongs to your _____, and cut down the _____ that is beside it" (NASB).

Gideon had already been told he would "deliver Israel from the power of Midian" (v.14). But his ministry wouldn't start there. Gideon was to lead a reformation beginning from the place where he'd opened his eyes that morning.

His own house.

That the age of the bull Gideon would slay correlated to the number of years Midian had ravaged Israel was no coincidence. This year, the eighth, would be the last—for both.

HEARTS TOWARD HOME

Gideon's first assignment seemed contrary to what the angel of the LORD had said to him earlier. Delivering his house from an idol wasn't the first logical step toward delivering Israel from Midian. But the former would be a required stepping stone to the latter. Until Israel was rid of her idols and her fidelity to them, external freedom from hardship would be at best temporary and superficial.

So Gideon's work would begin in the circle closest to him and spread outward from there. The journey of fulfilling our divine purpose will almost always follow this same pattern. Take note of the journey of Gideon's calling.

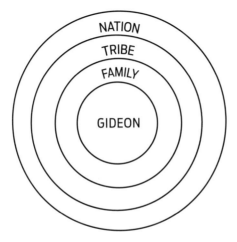

Why do you think Gideon beginning his work in this way was critical to Israel's overarching success?

For more study: Note who responded when Gideon blew his trumpet to rally his countrymen for battle in Judges 6:34-35. See the outward progression of his influence—throughout his tribe, then throughout the nation.

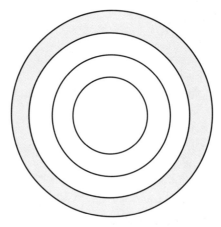

Record your initials in the smallest of the circles above. In the slightly larger circles, write the next two spheres of influence in your life—the people or environments closest to you.

Prayerfully consider those you just wrote in the chart. What is God asking you to do in relation to them? Why do you think people often avoid these circles?

Choosing to do our primary work in the smaller, less noticeable spheres and devote our best gifts there is often a foreign thought to us. We usually want to jump from the center directly to the perimeter of impact, skipping over the areas most closely connected to us. The result? A life and calling that eventually implode, caving in upon their shoddy, unstable structure.

God had strategically set Gideon in this family, in this tribe, and in this valley for a reason. He fully intended to call and equip Gideon to affect his closest relationships before moving on to something and someone else.

The priority and preeminence of serving those in the sphere closest to us is seen throughout Scripture. When Abraham was chosen by God to be the father of Israel, he was given instructions for what his first tasks should be.

Turn to Genesis 18:19. In your own words, what did God tell Abraham to concentrate on prior to experiencing the fulfillment of His promises?

Centuries later, as Jesus' disciples were ushered into the age of the church, God gave them a unique power to function on His behalf, and then clearly outlined the course their ministry was to follow.

From Acts 1:8 below, underline the three spheres of influence mentioned, and then record them in order below:

1.

2.

3.

But you will receive power when the Holy Spirit has come upon you; and you shall be My witnesses both in Jerusalem, and in all Judea and Samaria, and even to the remotest part of the earth.
ACTS 1:8, NASB

The disciples were in Jerusalem when they received these instructions from Jesus. They were to focus on the ministry to be done where they were standing even as they began moving outward on mission. Start inward, move outward.

First things first. Both for Gideon and for us.

IT'S HARDER AT HOME

Gideon had been reared in an idol-worshiping family. His own father was the keeper of the Baal altar in their town of Ophrah.

Answer the following questions, using Judges 6:27 as a guide:

1. Did Gideon do what God asked him to?

2. How did he do it?

3. Why did he do it this way?

A Baal altar was found at Megiddo that measured some twenty-six feet across and four and a half feet high. Made of many stones, cemented together by mud, such an altar would constitute an immense task to destroy and carry away.[1]

Often, like in Gideon's case, our smaller spheres of influence are not easier to contend with just because they are smaller. On the contrary, some of the most difficult and intimidating opportunities to walk in God's calling come when we are staring in the faces of those who know us best and whom we love the most.

Consider how Gideon must have felt tearing down what his father had spent his lifetime building, teaching, and defending. With each stone that he and his servants dismantled, another layer of the ideology that had overrun his family came unglued. This overnight idol-demolishing wasn't affecting some random town and family he would never see again. This was a task he'd feel, see, and endure the consequences of every day from that point on.

When the Christian daughter chooses to evangelize her non-Christian parents …

When the godly wife chooses to set an example for her unsaved spouse …

When the teenager seeks to impact his pagan school environment …

When the coworker tries to influence her friends on the job …

The stakes are often much higher when the mission field is so personal.

I've darkened the outlying circle in the earlier diagram, because what lies ahead in your journey is not nearly as critical as where you are right now. Wherever you are now is where you are meant to serve now. These innermost circles are often the ones that offer the least amount of recognition. This is why so many people try to circumvent them. And yet your greatest impact will be done here—in the ordinary rhythms of your daily living.

Following God wholeheartedly within these up-close loops of faith will often cause you an internal uneasiness and daily faithfulness that cannot be escaped just because it's 5 p.m. and the workday is over. It's easier to stand on a platform and teach people we may never see again than to walk with our own children, friends, and loved ones in accountability and discipleship. But these spheres encompass the heart of true ministry.

Begin to clarify who the people in your primary sphere of influence should be. Refuse to search for significance in another place if you've bypassed any near and necessary steps in the journey God has for you.

Pray for a courageous faith and holy boldness to start where you are. He'll give it to you.

Take a moment to soak in what God has taught you so far. How have you been challenged? How have you been encouraged? Journal your thoughts and spend some time talking to God as you close this week of our study.

TODAY I LEARNED:

Nehemiah

We often hear of Nehemiah in the context of leadership. He showed strength, intelligence, boldness, and endurance as he rallied the Israelites to rebuild the wall in Jerusalem. He stood fast in his calling because he knew the gracious hand of God was on him (2:8,18). Nehemiah was a great leader because he followed the greatest Leader.

The events in the Book of Nehemiah took place around 444 B.C. while Artaxerxes I was king of Persia. The Jewish people had been given permission to return to Jerusalem after Persia conquered the Babylonians who had held the Jews in exile. Not only were the Jews allowed to return to Jerusalem, they were given permission to rebuild.

Nehemiah began his journey of faithfulness as the cupbearer of the king. While serving in this capacity, Nehemiah learned that the Jewish remnant in Israel was in trouble. The wall around Jerusalem was still a pile of rubble, providing no protection from enemy nations and leaving the people in disgrace.

Upon hearing the news, Nehemiah wept. He mourned for several days, praying to "the great and awe-inspiring God who keeps his gracious covenant with those who love him and keep his commands" (1:5).

Nehemiah did not approach the situation lightly. He did not immediately run out, grab a hammer, and start rebuilding. He showed patience, compassion, and wisdom. Only after proper preparation did Nehemiah lead his people to rebuild.

Nehemiah shows us what it means to be a servant leader. We see a heart that reflects God's—a heart that breaks with love for His people. We see what it looks like to be called to do big and uncomfortable things for God's glory. And in this story, we see our compassionate God working things together in His perfect time, rebuilding what has been torn down.

Like Nehemiah, we, too, are called to be set apart, compassionate, and faithful to our great and awe-inspiring God.

ABOUT NEHEMIAH: A HEART THAT CAN BREAK

Originally published in 2012, *Nehemiah: A Heart That Can Break* is a 7-session women's Bible study by Kelly Minter. This study challenges women to let God break their hearts for a hurting, lost world and move them in compassion to lead people to Jesus.

ABOUT KELLY MINTER

Kelly Minter is an author, speaker, songwriter, and singer. She is passionate about women discovering Jesus Christ through the pages of Scripture. So whether it's through a song, study, or spoken word, Kelly's desire is to authentically express Christ to the women of this generation. In a culture where so many are hurting and broken, she loves to share about the healing and strength of Christ through the Bible's truth. Kelly writes extensively and speaks and leads worship at women's conferences, retreats, and events.

WEEK
2

Come Together

I DECIDED TO START CANNING TOMATOES SO I COULD READILY ACCESS THE FLAVORS OF SUMMER IN TASTELESS MONTHS LIKE FEBRUARY; AT LEAST THIS WAS WHY I INITIALLY THOUGHT I WANTED TO CAN. I KNOW YOU CAN BUY CANS OF TOMATOES AT THE GROCERY STORE YEAR-ROUND—MY FRIENDS REMIND ME OF THIS ALL THE TIME—BUT WHERE'S THE HEART AND PERSONAL RISK IN THIS?

Like cooking, canning requires a certain commitment, only the stakes are much higher when you can. If you get canning wrong you can end up with a funny little bacteria called botulism, meaning you could die over a plate of linguini. This terrified me, which is why I went for broke and bought a pressure canner—a large aluminum pot that can reach superheated temperatures and quite possibly build up enough steam to launch a rocket to Uruguay. Ironically this life-threatening pot is a weapon with which you can waltz right out of the cookware aisle.

The first time I tried out my pressure canner I watched for steam to escape through a small vent pipe on the lid, at which point I placed a small pressure regulator on top of it. You're supposed to wait until the steam inside the canner builds up enough pressure to move the regulator back and forth, and, incidentally, this takes more time than you might think. Figuring I'd probably botched the whole procedure I decided to start over and pulled the regulator off. This was a grave error. What transcended was a release of steam that shot like a laser beam to the ceiling in a shrieking howl that threw me to the kitchen floor.

After that little number I put the weight back on and finally it started moving in—what was supposed to be—a "gentle, rocking motion," though mine was rattling like a train was about to plow through the lid. I cowered from a distance, watching the whole contraption hoot and holler on my stove top, wondering if the dangers of pressure canning had surpassed the dangers of botulism—what's a little bacteria compared to blowing myself up in my own home?

This was just the processing part. Don't get me started on the bushels of tomatoes I'd hauled in from the farmers' market—the ones I'd blanched, dipped in ice water, peeled, cored, and funneled into a jar all by myself. My friends suddenly had "other" things to do like sweep under their beds. Hundreds of tomatoes in wooden baskets overtook my dining room table and countertops, plenty for what I perceived could keep all of Italy cranking for at least a couple months. It wasn't until I checked the directions, and realized it takes about forty-five pounds of tomatoes to make approximately seven quarts of sauce, that I began to question the path my life was on.

It was then that I roughly priced out my hard and soft costs: pressure canner, canning supplies, tomatoes, lemons for lemon juice, salt, suffering, and overall trauma. Based on rough configurations my jars of tomatoes came to about $73 a piece, if you keep health insurance out of it.

Further troubling was that I didn't process the first seven jars correctly (add additional "learning-curve expense"). The lids sealed so they were most likely "safe" to eat, but tossing them felt like prudence so I set them aside. The next day my exceedingly helpful friend April came over and, without me knowing, put away all the jars in the pantry, in other words mixing good jars with possibly tainted ones. This created a scenario called Tomato Russian Roulette—don't know if you've ever heard of it—which we played until all the tomatoes had been eaten.

Whenever I opened my pantry I happily stared at the rows of jewel-red jars, despite the underlying possibility of severe illness. Each one was like a little quart of gold to me, though more expensive than gold mind you. They made me feel settled and homey, like I lived in the old days when people used to sway on their porch swings while shucking corn and talking about how the neighbors' chickens got out of their coup. Popping open a lid was like freeing the taste of August into the dead of winter, and this lured guests into my home. It was these guests who made all my canning toils disappear

into soups, sauces, and chili, especially when they would say something like, "This is the best sauce ever!" And I would say, "Oh, it's probably because I can my own tomatoes. It's nothing really." Then we'd sit down and eat and converse and share life together. And I would totally forget I'd almost died.

It took some analyzing to discover, but the real reason I started canning is because I'm deeply relational. In the end, canning was about dinner and dinner was about conversation and community and togetherness.

Which is why the week we're about to explore is one of my favorites because all types of people—young, rich, city folk, farmers, old, rulers, servants, merchants, priests, and women—will join Nehemiah in a grand endeavor they will undertake together. It will make all of Nehemiah's solitary praying, petitioning, and assessing mean so much more. Because the trip he is about to take to Jerusalem was never really about stones or gates but about the community those fortifications would protect. Be it canning tomatoes or building walls, it's all about the people.

ASSESSING THE NEED

Summer nears, enticing me with visions of succulent heirloom tomatoes lining the side of my house in a valiant row of edible architecture that gets the perfect amount of sun and protective shade. I have plans for squash and zucchini, though I hear if you have even half a plan for squash they will proliferate and overtake your life—if there's ever a shortage of squash in the world, the end is near. I would like to pluck onions from the ground that I can use in that evening's meal or simply add to the previously harvested mound that sits in a dark cool space in my pantry. I see shoots of garlic hanging in my kitchen, their stalks wound together in culinary braids. I have dreams of raised beds made from nontreated railroad ties that are equal parts productive and aesthetic.

Of course all this is vain imagination. Right now I have nothing but a cleared backyard and a book called *The Vegetable Gardener's Bible* my friend Lisa gave me. But I'm earmarking pages and researching exciting things like compost piles. I'm watching documentaries on eating locally, and with each new slice of information I'm carried closer to my imaginary garden becoming a reality where all will be welcome to come by for squash.

Executing one's vision demands thoughtful assessment and proper planning. Though my plans for shiny eggplants don't compare with Nehemiah's zeal to rebuild the wall of Jerusalem, reach with me out of kindness. Nehemiah had a vision to rebuild the walls, but how to execute the vision required research and investigation. He needed to know what he was up against before he could unveil his plan. He had some assessments to make, which I want you to read about in Nehemiah 2:11-20.

What was Nehemiah doing in the middle of the night (see v. 13)?

A working picture of Jerusalem's walls will help us see the parts Nehemiah scouted during his first few days in Jerusalem. Though we don't know precisely where everything was located, scholars have come up with some pretty good renditions. See the map on page 55, which you will complete on day 2 this week.

Nehemiah knew that the wall had to be rebuilt, but until he assessed the damage and examined the degree of brokenness he couldn't begin to know what that job would entail. Jesus speaks to this same principle when describing the cost of being His disciple in Luke 14:28-33.

PERSONAL TAKE: Reread Nehemiah 2:16. Why do you think Nehemiah kept his mission a secret at first?

What might have happened if he'd told of his idea too early?

PERSONAL RESPONSE: What has God put on your heart to do? Write down passages of Scripture that come to mind, longings you have for others, people you want to reach out to.

Nehemiah had been the wise caretaker of the plan God put in his heart. He had fostered and sculpted it during his four months of prayer and planning, he had delicately laid it before the king, and now he was ushering it into Jerusalem under the tight cover of his heart. He would keep it a secret until it became clear that the time had arrived for him to unveil his plan. As David Kidner said so perfectly, "He would have lost this [initiative] if he had been exposing half-formed ideas piecemeal to every acquaintance."[1] Um, why does it sound like Kidner has met me?

I am excellent at keeping a secret someone has entrusted to me, but when God has laid something on my heart that I am excited about, I tend to wing it out there sometimes too quickly. I can be a glutton for immediate feedback and other people's reactions. Discussing things over with trustworthy people is a wonderful gift, but sometimes God drops a dream in our hearts that we must pray over and develop, that we must cultivate by His Word and direction before we share it with others. Here we get a beautiful example from Nehemiah who nurtured a seed of dis - grace

vision into a fully recognizable bloom, before making it known. In verses 17-18 Nehemiah revealed his plan to the people.

> What compelling reason did he give at the end of verse 17 for why the wall should be rebuilt?

This is exactly what upset Nehemiah so much in 1:3. It wasn't just the suffering of the people but the disgrace of a city that, according to Psalm 48:2, was supposed to be the joy of the whole earth, the city of the Great King! Things were not the way they were supposed to be. Certainly we live in a different time, even under a different covenant. But the principles carry beyond Nehemiah's day. Disgraces, tragedies, and abuses take place all around us—things that should not be. God's church is to work at setting things right as we seek His kingdom here on earth.

As Nehemiah's heart broke over Jerusalem's disgrace, ours should break for the disgrace of the poor, abused, abandoned, and lost. Especially for those who may not appear disgraced in their put-together outfits and sewn-up facades but who are tormented with shame on the inside. As New Testament believers we recognize that our task is not to rebuild the physical city of God's dwelling place but to bring restoration to people's hearts through Jesus Christ who takes away our sin and shame.

> God no longer dwells in a physical temple but where?
> (See 1 Cor. 3:16-17; Col. 1:27.)

> Have you ever forced a plan or a dream that, in retrospect, you realized God's hand wasn't on? If so, what did you learn from this experience?

Nehemiah had to convince the people that rebuilding the wall was a worthy cause, and he didn't do this from a distance. In 2:17: "You see the trouble we are in. ... Come, let us rebuild" (HCSB). Nehemiah didn't merely send help from Persia, but he chose to share in their suffering and recovery process. We can't miss this extreme display of sacrifice as we consider how we are identifying with the poor and suffering in our own lives.

For such a massive undertaking, Nehemiah had to make the case that Yahweh was unmistakably involved. How did he do this in verse 18?

How had God already demonstrated His involvement (see v. 8)?

Nehemiah knew without a doubt that God had given him the vision to rebuild and His gracious hand was upon him with every step. This makes all the difference when tackling something that's beyond our natural strength because if we're not assured of God's presence we will find a thousand reasonable opportunities to turn back.

How did the people respond to Nehemiah's plan in verse 18?
☐ reluctantly
☐ with skepticism
☐ favorably
☐ with indifference

Reread verses 19-20 and fill in the missing information about Nehemiah's prominent enemies.

_____, the Arab; Tobiah, the _____; and _____, the Horonite.

We'll learn more about these characters in the days to come, but that opposition would follow the Jews' decision to rebuild the walls of the city, where God's Name dwelt, is no surprise. For now, let's look at Nehemiah's response to them.

What did Nehemiah say God would do?

What did he say he and the Jews would do?

True/False: Nehemiah encouraged the opposition to take part in rebuilding if only they stopped their attacks.

I love Nehemiah's response as much for what he didn't say as for what he did. I can't believe he didn't whip out his building permit from King Artaxerxes like an FBI agent flashes his badge. But when Nehemiah spoke, he only credited the God of heaven for his future success (see 1:5). He saw God's hand as far superior in moving Jerusalem forward and in dealing with Sanballat, Tobiah, and Geshem. Nehemiah didn't mention his military escort or the backing he'd received from Persia; only God's favor, God's people, and the distinction of Jerusalem. Brilliant.

PERSONAL RESPONSE: In what situation do you desperately need God's hand? Where are you leaning on your own resources?

As I think about Nehemiah's response to opposition, I think of my desperate need for God in all areas of my life. I don't write a lot about my singleness, at least not in the sense of it being an incomplete stage of life, or worse yet, a nonmedical disease. (Plus, it tends to set off a frantic alarm in women who suddenly have an unruly urge to set me up with their son, cousin, or uncle they haven't seen in fifteen years, but who really loves the Lord. I write in love.) But in the last few months I have become very aware of how much I take care of myself.

My dream was never to do life without someone committed to walking alongside me until death do us part. I have friends who are as tight as family. My life is filled to the brim with joy and adventure, but only a man can fill the roll of a man in my life. Some days I wake up and say, "Lord, be my husband, my father, my brother," even though I have the best father and brother ever; they just don't live close enough to mow my lawn. I long for the faith of Nehemiah who looked the opposition dead in the eye and said, "I've got God." And, by the way, He trumps everything.

CITY GATES,
SOUL GATES

When projects turn overwhelming and the obstacles loom, camaraderie rolls the windows down and gets the breeze blowing, reminding us that everyone's in this thing together. During my winter trip to the Amazon I had the joy of working with a team and benefiting from everyone's gifts and personalities. My dad taught the jungle pastors on the veranda while my friends Warren and Mike oversaw the builders. Now, my father is a man of the Scriptures and an exquisite teacher, but please don't allow him to touch a hammer. If your toilet overflows, he will tell you to pray about it. Conversely, none of us could have preached for five hours at a time without a note, fielding questions with humble ease from phenomenal men of a different culture.

While builders built and teachers taught, my friend Jaye made home visits, sidestepping religious and cultural minefields, moving straight to the hearts of perfect strangers with a graceful authority that would astound you. Come evening, Brad, dropped his drill for a gaggle of little boys and girls who followed him around like the Pied Piper. At any moment you might have seen Juliet, my dear English friend, drawing tanned, weary hands to her chest, praying comforting prayers over women desperate for a touch from God. Occasionally I would pick up my guitar and lead deep and theologically complex songs like Father Abraham (left foot, right foot, turn around …). So few can do what I do.

In the end, we all made way for one another's gifts. Joy upon joy came from doing it together.

> Discuss your best experience working with a team. Whose skills and personality did you especially appreciate? What did everyone accomplish by working together?

Today we enter a new phase in the Book of Nehemiah. One scholar commented that chapters 1–2 describe the "innovation process" while chapters 3–7:4 describe the "community development process."[2] Up until this point Nehemiah had been defining his vision and preparing for its execution, but now the time had come for the work to begin. This he could not do alone.

Take time to read Nehemiah 3:1-15.

Chapter 3 mentions at least forty sections of the wall, but today we'll primarily focus on the gates discussed in the first fifteen verses. We will gather geographical information and identify a few notable people, reminding ourselves that this was a real wall built by real people.

Look at the map on page 55. In the blanks, fill in the name of each gate and tower according to the given reference.

What phrase is repeatedly used to describe the repairs made to each gate? (Phrase found in vv. 3,6,13-15.)

I didn't notice the repetition of this phrase until months into studying Nehemiah. Once recognizing it, I had to ponder its profound significance: Little is as important to a city as guarding the places where people come and go. Jerusalem's walls meant nothing without fortified gates—every door, bolt, and bar had to be scrutinized and secured. This led me to think about the "gates" in my life, what I allow to enter my seeing and hearing, even what I taste and touch. I thought about the gates mothers and fathers are in charge of overseeing for the sake of their children. The question became, "What am I allowing in and out?"

Have you ever wondered if "mindless entertainment" might actually be a wide-open gate in your life by which many hurtful and deceiving ideas are sliding straight into your thinking? What about the friendships you keep, the magazines you read, the conversations in which you choose to engage? Are your doors open to the uplifting, truth-telling, and life-giving, or to what corrodes your soul? All day long we choose what goes in and out of our hearts and minds, and if you're like me there are some doors, bars, and bolts that need tightening.

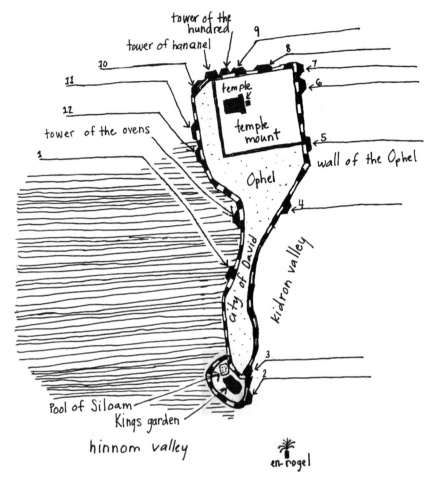

tower of the hundred

tower of hananel

9

8

10

7

11

6

temple

12

temple mount

tower of the ovens

1

5

wall of the Ophel

Ophel

4

city of David

kidron valley

3

2

Pool of Siloam

Kings garden

hinnom valley

en-rogel

ON THE MAP: Fill in the gates of Jerusalem as numbered, beginning with those mentioned in Nehemiah 2:13-15. Note several locations are approximate or subject to debate.

1. Valley Gate
2. Dung Gate
3. Fountain Gate
4. Water Gate
5. Horse Gate
6. Inspection Gate
7. East Gate
8. Gate of the Guard
9. Sheep Gate
10. Fish Gate
11. Gate of Jeshanah
12. Gate of Ephraim

PERSONAL RESPONSE: What "gates" in your life need reinforcement? Explain. (See Eph. 6:10-18 for further meditation.)

Just as the Jews were called to guard their city, so we are called to guard our hearts. Keep considering this connection as we continue to study the rebuilding of Jerusalem's walls and gates.

> Nehemiah 3:5 breaks from the consistently positive narrative of eager workers and mentions a resistant group. Who were they?
> ☐ servants
> ☐ nobles
> ☐ women and children
> ☐ foreigners

Tekoa (home of the prophet Amos) was located southeast of Bethlehem near the area controlled by Geshem. These nobles may have feared getting involved in the work based on their close proximity to enemy territory, though we can't be sure. In any case, it's discouraging to see that not everyone was onboard though a good leader understands that the work can't be stopped because a few oppose or refuse to be involved. I'm that person who doesn't like to move forward without everyone's support and approval, but this can be idealistic and maybe a tiny bit codependent. The Lord helped break me of this during a difficult situation where being obedient to Him meant walking alone.

> PERSONAL REFLECTION: What about you? Is it hard for you to move forward without everyone's support or approval? Why or why not?

> What trades are associated with the following men (v. 8)?
> Uzziel: _____ Hananiah: _____

Many engaged in the work based on family or geographical ties, but some came together based on their specific trades. People who have refined their skills fascinate me because the investment of developing one is so steep; years of studying and practice go into honing a craft. You can't buy the skill of piano playing like you can buy the piano.

> PERSONAL REFLECTION: If you could have any trade or skill, what would it be and why?

Though we should all be intent on using our specific gifts and trades for the service of God, sometimes we have to meet a need whether we're suited for the job or not. This was true of the goldsmith, perfumers, and merchants (mentioned later) who worked to rebuild Jerusalem, even though this type of work had little to do with their skill set. They saw a need, and they took their place on the wall.

Look back at verse 12. With whom did Shallum repair his section of the wall? His …
□ servants
□ sons
□ daughters
□ nobles

This is a profound mention given the cultural mores of the day. According to David J. A. Clines' book on Nehemiah, "The daughters were mentioned only because Shallum had no sons. There is no reason to think they were the only women involved in the construction."[3]

For further explanation, read Numbers 27:1-11. According to this passage, who would inherit the name and property of a father who had no sons?

According to Numbers 36:8-12, what were the daughters who received the inheritance to then do?

This scene of Shallum and his daughters working together to rebuild the city of God needs no embellishment. It is simply beautiful.

PERSONAL RESPONSE: If you have children, how can you involve them in missional projects? If you don't have children, how can you involve your nieces, nephews, or the children of close friends?

Carrie writes about how she is already involving her four-year-old, Finley. "It is so important to me for my kids to understand God's grace and have a thankful heart. We thank God every night in our prayers for giving us a bed and a house to sleep in. We talk about how some people don't have what we have. A group of us had the chance to help our church with a program called 'Room At The Inn' which gives men a bed and a warm meal for the night. It was important for me to walk my son Fin around the room where all the cots were laid out beforehand. We talked about how the men who would use them did not have a home right now but that God loves them just like He loves all of us. I pray that this makes a visual impact on him and how we need to appreciate the bed that we take for granted every night. We need to daily look for types of teaching opportunities for our kids (and for us)!"

> PERSONAL REFLECTION: Regardless of where you are, as you end today's lesson ponder 1 Corinthians 12:1-11. What gifts has the Spirit given you?

SIDE BY SIDE

Sometimes it takes a catastrophe to meet your neighbor. When Nashville was pummeled by a hundred-year flood, streams of us trickled out of our houses and onto the streets. When struck by a shared hardship, unrelated people can bond in an instant over the common goal of recovery. During the flood cleanup, while rebuilding a stranger's house, I met more people from my home church than I had in the last eight years of Sunday morning attendance. With four services and minimal time between each, you're not afforded as much time to build relationships as when you're sweeping your paintbrush steadily against the trim and the person next to you is rolling, and suddenly you discover you both love real estate. Since the flood I can walk into my church at any service and find myself waving to Scott and Donna, Mildred and Gene, Andy, Tyler, Cindy, Chris, and Kitty. The funny thing is I didn't meet any of them in the walls of church but in a stranger's house doing church. Side by side.

> Pray over today's study time. Ask God to reveal Himself to you.

Today's passage moves us from the western and northern parts of the wall to the eastern side. You will notice that it reads differently from yesterday's portion of Nehemiah because the landmarks are mostly personal houses and buildings instead of gates.

> Read Nehemiah 3:16-32 and tally the number of times "next to him," "after him," or "beside him" are used. (Try not to miss the content for the counting.)

> What strikes you most about today's reading?

> Verses 20-21 tell us that Baruch and Meremoth helped make repairs on the high priest Eliashib's house. Looking back at verse 1, where had Eliashib been working?

> After him Baruch son of Zabbai diligently repaired another section, from the angle of the door of the house of Eliashib the high priest.
> NEHEMIAH 3:20, HCSB

Eliashib's unique position as a high priest required that he focus his attention on the strategically important area of the northern wall which was close to the temple. He didn't have the luxury (or he laid down the luxury) of staying home and working on the wall across from his own house. Whereas many could do the work of repairing the wall near their homes, the dedication of towers and gates required the special office of a high priest. I really love the idea of Baruch and Meremoth repairing what is of particular interest to Eliashib while he was away offering his services to the Lord on a unique part of the wall. While Eliashib was serving God, Baruch and Meremoth were serving God by serving Eliashib.

What adjective is used to describe the work of Baruch?

This translated word appears only here in Nehemiah. It means *to burn, to be earnest.* We are all called to be compassionate, kind, and zealous for the things of God (see Col. 3:12; Rom. 12:11), but our life experiences and gifts will naturally cause us to care more deeply about some things than others.

My friend Warren, the builder I mentioned yesterday, has a grandson with special needs. Barring a miracle from the Lord, his grandchild will never sit up on his own, nor will he ever be able to feed himself. Because of this difficult experience, and because of Christ's heart in Warren, he sponsors children with special needs all over the world. Like Baruch, he literally burns with compassion for them.

My friend Angie Smith (author of *I Will Carry You*) lost her beloved daughter Audrey within a few hours of giving birth. In the wake of this devastating hardship, she writes, "Too much is happening in the world for us to sit back and ignore what we are being called to, and for me that stems from my love of children."[4] I don't know what you're zealous for, but whatever it is, work at it earnestly. Because as I now like to say, "If it's not Baruch, you might want to fix it."

PERSONAL RESPONSE: In matters relating to God's kingdom, what are you most zealous about? What makes your heart burn?

If you currently feel numb and dull and can't put your finger on anything, <u>ask</u> <u>God to create in you a kingdom passion.</u> This is His will so you can feel confident praying for it.

Earlier you kept count of the references of "next to," "after," and "beside" him. How many did you come up with?

Though the catalogue of names listed in chapter 3 may seem tedious at first, it represents an extraordinary feat of organization and accomplishment and displays a beautiful picture of God's people working together to accomplish God's purposes. They did it next to one another in a display of community that makes me freshly happy our God has not called us to serve Him alone.

PERSONAL TAKE: Here is a short list of names pulled from chapter 3. Fill in their vocations in the following chart. What inspires you the most about their diversity? Respond below the chart.

NAME	VOCATION
Eliashib (see v. 1)	High Priest
Uzziel (see v. 8)	
Hananiah (see v. 8)	Perfumer
Rephaiah (see v. 9)	
Pedaiah (see vv. 25-26)	
Shemaiah (see v. 29)	

I am amazed at the organization behind getting all of these different types of people to work together with common intention and efficiency. Though a testament to Nehemiah's leadership, we don't get a "how-to" as much as a "he-did." What we will continue to discover about Nehemiah is that he did it because the hand of his great God was upon him. One thing you may have noticed is that although Nehemiah 3 contains great diversity, culturally speaking it was homogeneous; everyone was a Jew, or a proselyte who had chosen to convert. Since the coming of Christ, this has drastically changed as the gospel has spread in extraordinary directions, reaching all manner of distinctive people.

Where did Jesus call His disciples to be witnesses (see Acts 1:8)?

Who can be in Christ according to Colossians 3:11?

Some of my richest, deepest, and most hysterically funny moments have been with people from other countries or people who are simply different from me. These relationships do more than keep me interested and entertained, they remind me of the universality of the gospel. When we come to "the wall" alongside believers who are vastly unique, our faith is deepened. Paul speaks to this gift of fellowship in 1 Thessalonians 3:10.

Fill in the blanks: "Night and day we pray most earnestly that we may see you again and _____ what is _____ in your _____" (NIV).

I love the New Living Translation, which says, "to fill the gaps in your faith," much like the people were filling in the gaps in the wall.

Who consistently supplies what is lacking in your faith? How so?

To me, one of the most freeing phrases in today's reading is "each in front of his own house" (v. 28, NIV, see also vv. 29-30). There is no question that we as the body of Christ have a responsibility to those living beyond our immediate spheres, and yet there is much work to be done right where we've been planted: in our work environments, communities, neighborhoods, schools, churches, and families. God may be calling you to serve in the places that are right in front of your own home! I love how scholar H. G. M. Williamson puts it: "It seems that Nehemiah allowed each group to be responsible, so far as possible, for the section of the wall in which *they had the greatest vested interest*—because it protected their home, place of business, or the like. ... [We need not] be disquieted if we find that it *comes most easily, and with the greatest sense of motivation, to channel those gifts in areas closest to our own concerns*" (emphasis added).[5]

Read 1 Corinthians 12:12-27, keeping Nehemiah 3 in mind. Let Paul's words encourage you as you consider how you are investing in the body of Christ. Respond below.

ENTER THE OPPOSITION

I've learned something significant about myself in the past few months: I hate confrontation more than meatloaf. It's been an unusual season of opposition that's made me long for someone to pass the reins off to, and if that person happens to be an attractive single man, well then chime the wedding bells. Until then the Lord is teaching me to trust Him as my Defender while making me tougher. Sometimes you have to draw back, keep quiet, and pray, but I'm learning that other times God asks you to get out there and stand your ground. Today and throughout the Book of Nehemiah we'll witness a biblical blend of both. Read Nehemiah 4:1-6.

What part of opposition bothers you the most? Why?

Up to now the enemies' threats have been more annoying than effective at interrupting the work. But this is the first time we're told that Sanballat had shown up in person, bringing his allies with him. When looking at our opposition it's helpful to understand the reason behind their angst.

According to verse 1, why were the Jews' enemies so upset?

Based on the multitude of enemies confronting the Jews, Jerusalem's situation brings fresh meaning to the phrase, "opposed on every side."

Sanballat was governor of Samaria which was to the north of Jerusalem.

Tobiah is believed to have held a high office in the land of Ammon, which sat to the east of Jerusalem. Geshem is thought to have ruled a host of Arabian tribes which ruled over Moab, Edom, and Arabia, which were Judah's neighbors to the east and south. The Ashdodites were the Jews' western neighbor.

PERSONAL RESPONSE: Think about a time when you felt attacked from every side. What did you learn from this season, and how did it affect your relationship with God?

Don't miss how angry and incensed Sanballat had become when he found out that the wall was progressing. The literal translation is to "become hot" and "be angry," and when used together in this particular form the intent is to relay intense, raging anger.[6] Sanballat's territory was being threatened by the promise of a restored Jerusalem, and when people are threatened they tend to go straight for the throat. Out of control rage does not heed reason or common courtesy, which is why Sanballat attacked the Jews where they were most vulnerable.

PERSONAL REFLECTION: Think about what half-truths leveled at you have hurt you the most. Why do you think the wounds that carry a shard of truth are the most painful?

Fill in Sanballat's missing word: What are those _____ Jews doing? (See Neh. 4:2.)

These fighting words stood to puree the Jews' confidence because they held just enough truth to be devastating.

Look up Deuteronomy 7:1,6-8, and answer the following:

True/False: The Israelites inherited the promised land because they were bigger and stronger than five of the seven nations they were told to drive out.

True/False: God chose Israel as His treasured possession, even though they were the fewest of all peoples.

In the entire Old Testament the word *pathetic* (HCSB) or *feeble* (NIV) appears only here, and Sanballat was the one to hurl it against God's people while his sidekick Tobiah tossed out jokes about a fox toppling a nine-foot thick wall. They remind me of the two old men from the Muppets® who wisecracked from the safety of their theater booth, only meaner. They had yet to shoot an arrow but the dart of words had been fired, and from Nehemiah's response in verses 4-5 we see that he and the Jews took it to heart, "Listen, our God, for *we are despised*" (emphasis added).

Words can be the most damaging thorns pressed into our hearts, often hurting far more than any physical blow. The Jews were well aware that they were not known for their size or strength; with opposing leaders and an army now forcefully reminding them of this, they needed to hear from God. So Nehemiah prayed.

In an escalating situation like this, prayer doesn't always feel like the fastest or most efficient solution. We're accustomed, even trained, to look to our resources first, wrack our brains, and at the very least Google® our problems for some immediate answers. We want quick remedies for our quandaries and our suffering. But this is where Nehemiah provides an encouraging example. God was always his first stop; action always followed, it never led. Look at the following three couplets of obedience and action: "So I prayed. 'If it pleases the king ... send me' " (2:4-5, HCSB). "The God of heaven is the One who will grant us success. We, His servants, will start building" (2:20, HCSB). "Listen, our God. ... So we rebuilt the wall. ... We prayed to our God and stationed a guard" (4:4-9, HCSB).

PERSONAL REFLECTION: Write about something to which you've applied your resources, brain power, or finances but haven't spent significant time praying about.

Will you commit to petitioning the Lord about this situation for at least the remainder of our study?

How did the people work according to Nehemiah 4:6?

The potential effectiveness of the verbal assaults stopping the work was diverted by prayer and the people's willingness to work with all their hearts. The Lord also had given them wisdom about how to proceed.

According to verse 6, how high did they build the wall, and how much of it was built to this height?

So instead of completing the sections that were easily coming along and leaving the more difficult chunks for later, they decided to get the whole wall to the halfway mark. This may have meant leaving certain portions that were well-along in order to fill the gaps that were leaving vulnerable holes. It was better for the whole wall to be shored up, even though incomplete, than to have fully built sections here and there while others lie disconnected. This feels like divine wisdom to me.

Had this wall been up to me, I would have held my megaphone shouting opposite directions like, "Let's finish up what's working and leave what's not working for later—chips and salsa at my house!" The way they chose to move forward really ministers to me right now because I am desperate for God's wisdom in some specific areas of my life. According to James 1:5, He gives it generously to those who ask.

If only this chapter ended right here with the Jews successfully rebuilding despite the intimidating insults of Sanballat, Tobiah, and the rest of them. But the story keeps going, and the enemies don't fatigue as easily as we'd hope. Continue reading verses 7-9.

After Israel's enemies saw that their verbal threats had gone unheeded, what new measures did they plot to undertake?

If damaging words cause us devastating pain, physical threats cause downright fear. If we need God's healing truth for the former, we need His physical defense for the latter. Now that Sanballat and company had upped the ante by threatening a physical attack, suddenly the work on the wall loomed large and unlikely. But Nehemiah responded with prayer—and a plan of action, which we are finding to be his *modus operandi*.

According to verse 9, what was Nehemiah's twofold response?

When major opposition comes our way, it's essential to know we're in the right place, doing the right thing. This will give us strength in our weariness and confidence in our fear. Nehemiah's vision wasn't shaken because he was convinced of what God had put in his heart to do. He knew what the Old Testament law and the prophets had to say about the significance of Jerusalem and therefore knew that his work was founded in accordance with God's will. After all, how could it not be of God to rebuild the very city where His name and people dwelled?

There have been times in my life when I've had difficulty discerning between opposition and God's discipline. Just because we're enduring a lot of hardship and onslaughts doesn't necessarily mean we're "suffering for doing good." Sometimes we're suffering for sticking our finger in the socket. When we're disobedient, natural consequences result, along with God's loving hand of discipline. Though these consequences may feel like enemy opposition, they're not the same thing.

On the other hand, you may be dead in the center of God's will and experiencing great attack, much like the Jews who were rebuilding the wall. If so, you must renew your confidence in God, even reminding Him of His promises to you, rehearsing the threats coming against you and your work: "They have thrown insults in the face of the builders" (v. 5, NIV). Take heart that you're on exactly the right road doing exactly the right thing.

How has knowing you were in the will of God helped you endure difficult opposition?

PERSONAL REFLECTION: If you're currently experiencing opposition, list the reasons why you still know you're on the right path. Use Scripture and confirmations the Lord has given you.

Look back at what you wrote about Nehemiah's twofold response in verse 9. What did he post day and night?

When it comes to our opposition it appears that a good defense is often as effective as a blistering offense. Being on guard can sometimes lack the excitement of blowing things up and shooting things out of cannons, it's more staid than being on offense. It's an easy concept to overlook as it tends to lack flash and commotion. No one likes to be the one to stay back. But the Bible has a lot to say about being on guard and what things warrant guarding.

Next to each Scripture reference, briefly write what we're to guard.
1 Timothy 6:20

Proverbs 4:23

Proverbs 4:13

Luke 12:1

There is a lot worth guarding in our lives, our hearts being one of the most significant. As you ponder what ways you need to shore up the protection over what God has entrusted to you, remember that He does not leave you alone. As we are guarding what He has entrusted to us, He is guarding us. "The peace of God, which surpasses every thought, will guard your hearts and minds in Christ Jesus" (Phil 4:7, HCSB).

REMOVING THE RUBBLE

After the Nashville flood I helped rebuild three homes, and during the process I learned a worthy lesson: The difference between building and rebuilding is rubble. Building starts with a clean slate and means new, freshly-scented materials. Rebuilding means maneuvering through piles of brick, metal, and junk before you get to hanging the stunning chandelier you found for half-price, the one God ordained for you to own before the foundation of the world. Read Nehemiah 4:10-15.

> Fill in the following from verse 10: "The _____ of the laborer fails, since there is so much _____. We will never be able to rebuild the wall" (HCSB).

Rebuilding means hauling stuff away and sorting through unruly piles, salvaging the keepers from the throwaways. While looking after the rebuilding of these homes, I got excited about the new granite countertops, the fresh paint, and the pristine cabinets. If I happened to be less riveted by the moldy drywall, water-logged couches, and trips to the dumpster, well then that was my problem, because this was a rebuild not a build. Rubble bridges the great divide between the two.

Rubble threatened to stop the laborers in Jerusalem dead in their tracks. Forget Sanballat's nasty threats; forget the Ammonites who were planning to fight against them. It was that exhausting rubble that just about took them down.

> What rubble in your life is presently the most discouraging and exhausting? (For example: finances, addictions, or relationships.)

The problem with rubble is that it hangs around well after the initial destruction. Though the attack on Jerusalem's walls had long since passed, the rubble was still present. But the Jews were dealing with it, and this is the good news. Similarly, it's important for us to deal with our personal rubble or we may find ourselves still climbing over it thirty years from now. How can we properly rebuild if we never address our rubble? Getting rid of rubble requires we do something.

> PERSONAL RESPONSE: What specific actions can you take to deal with your rubble? It may include seeking counsel, asking for help, or requesting accountability.

In addition to dealing with their own rubble, the Jews also contended with their enemies.

> What new and harrowing threat did the enemy launch? (See v. 11.)
> □ We will take them captive.
> □ We will think up more jokes about their wall.
> □ We will kill them.
> □ All of the above.
>
> What group of well-meaning people repeated this threat over and over to the laborers? (See v. 12.)

You may remember that King Artaxerxes had officially authorized the Jews to rebuild Jerusalem's walls, so the question naturally arises, How can their enemies do this? This is illegal! One thing I'm beginning to understand is that not everyone cares about what's legal or not, what's right or wrong. It's possible that Sanballat and his allies thought if they acted quickly enough there would be little the king of Persia could do.

Or perhaps they were hoping the king's authorization would eventually be reversed, as had happened before.

> What was ordered in Ezra 4:21-24?

Most of the Jews working on the wall in Nehemiah's day probably lived through the decree in Ezra. They had already experienced the despair of their work being stopped. When we've experienced past hardship we can easily let that precedent rule our present. We can all imagine the roads the Jews' minds may have taken them down during these trying threats. They may have viewed defeat as a foregone conclusion.

Jews from the surrounding areas turned into ancient-day re-Tweeters of Sanballat's threats (see Neh. 4:12). These concerned relatives and villagers knew that anyone who left the wall and returned to their towns would no longer be in trouble. That's why they urged the workers "time and again" to come home.[7]

You can imagine the scene: The perfume-maker's mother scurries into town and says, "Come off the wall, Son. They're going to kill you! Come back to your potentially lucrative trade; Chanel No. 5 hasn't been invented yet!" Or maybe Shallum's brother traveled in and said, "You're being reckless with my nieces! Haven't you heard the threat? Get them off the wall." Or what about the friends of the priests? "Eliashib! What use is your priesthood if you're dead?"

I believe the Jews from the surrounding areas were loving and concerned citizens, but they had lost sight of what was most important: The successful rebuild of Jerusalem. Even well-meaning people can unintentionally draw us away from God's will in our lives.

> Nehemiah, however, had not forgotten what God had put in his heart to do. So instead of succumbing to the threats and stopping the work, what did he propose in verse 13?

> Write out Nehemiah's quote in verse 14.

Nehemiah prescribed a very specific remedy for their fear: "Remember the great and awe-inspiring Lord" (HCSB). The laborers found themselves at the wearying halfway point that coincided with dizzying threats from their enemies that were being emphasized by their fellow townsfolk. The workers were discouraged, exhausted, and afraid.

PERSONAL REFLECTION: Given this information, why do you think Nehemiah's appeal to fight for their families and homes was particularly wise?

PERSONAL RESPONSE: What trying situation has caused you to dig extra deep because it threatened a family member or loved one? Explain.

I love that Nehemiah stationed family members together while reminding them of who it was they were fighting for in the first place. After all, this project wasn't about abstract notions or lifeless stone; this project was about people. And to each mother, father, or child, it was about his or her people.

Who are your people who God has asked you to fight for? List their names and pray over each one.

PERSONAL TAKE: What does verse 15 say God did to Sanballat and company's plot? What do you think this means, since we don't have a direct reference to God's intervening?

Read Nehemiah 4:16-23.

Fill in the blanks from verse 16: "_____ _____ _____, half of my men did the work while the other half held spears, shields, bows, and armor" (HCSB).

The Jews went back to business, but they never went back to business as usual. Because of the increasing threats of their enemies, they couldn't return to work the same way as before. Only half could do the work of building, while half now did the work of providing protection. If your job was to carry materials, you could no longer use both hands because one of them needed to have a weapon in it. If you were a builder, you had the extra weight of a sword strapped to your side.

And you could no longer just be a workman by day, you had to also be a guard by night. This'll knock the whistle-while-you-work right out of a person.

I wonder if you've had a "From this day on …" experience and how it has changed your life. Perhaps life hasn't resumed to the place you had hoped it would, and maybe you've had to resolve to doing some things differently. But despite what you've had to change, one thing will always remain constant: "Our God will fight for us!" (v. 20, HCSB).

> PERSONAL REFLECTION: What does this promise, given throughout the Bible, mean to you personally?

This has been a really interesting week of study for me, and I hope it's been as thought-provoking for you. I have a better grasp on the importance of teamwork and what it means for us as New Testament believers. I can more readily see how the excitement over a thrilling, even God-ordained, project can wane after verbal assaults and physical threats. How the rubble can get flat overwhelming, because let's face it, most of us are doing more rebuilding than building in life. How fear can pluck from the roots up the stuff God's put in your heart to do. And how even well-meaning loved ones can rehearse the reasons as to why what you're doing is not a good idea anymore.

I'm inspired by Nehemiah's unrelenting belief and trust in God, knowing that He would fulfill the vision He had given him. Without this kind of authoritative resolve, whoever would have followed him? As the apostle Paul said, "He who calls you is faithful, who also will do it" (1 Thess. 5:24, HCSB).

Esther

We don't know a lot about Esther's personality. We don't know if she was an introvert or an extrovert, if she liked sweet snacks or salty, or if she preferred to be called Esther or Hadassah. We do know she acted with courage when courage was required. She risked everything to save her people, God's people, from persecution.

The events in the Book of Esther took place around 483 B.C. when King Xerxes (your translation may say King Ahasuerus) was king of Persia. After the Babylonian captivity, the Israelites were scattered. Altough King Cyrus, the first king of Persia, conquered Babylon and set forth an edict allowing the Jewish people to return home, many of the Israelites remained in captivity, having assimilated to Persian culture by that time.

The Book of Esther is unique in that it never mentions God directly. However, the providence of God is clearly seen in its pages. The book is also known as The Megillah and is still read aloud each Purim (the annual Jewish holiday celebrating the events that unfold in the story of Esther).

Esther was a young, orphaned Jewish girl raised by her cousin Mordecai and taken to the palace of King Xerxes to compete to be queen of Persia. She won the king's affections and was chosen for the royal position of queen.

We see God's providence in her life, as she is placed in the palace "for such a time as this" (4:14). When the Israelite people were threatened with destruction, she used her influence on the king to save them.

Esther leveraged her position and influence for God's glory. She risked everything, including her very life, to do what was right, to act in faithful obedience to God.

Esther's example challenges us to do the same. As a young girl thrust into a seat of power, she showed her faith and trust in God. We are all called to use our influence and power (whatever form it may take) to give God glory. We are all called to take risks, to trust in His sovereignty, and to remain faithful "for such a time as this."

ABOUT ESTHER: IT'S TOUGH BEING A WOMAN

Originally published in 2008, *Esther: It's Tough Being a Woman* is a 10-session women's Bible study by Beth Moore. Through this study you will learn strong lessons of faith, providence, and hope to equip you to live courageously "for such a time as this."

ABOUT BETH MOORE

Beth Moore is an author and Bible teacher of best-selling Bible studies and books for women. She is the founder of Living Proof Ministries and speaker at Living Proof Live women's events across the U.S. Beth's mission is to guide women everywhere into a richer, more fulfilling relationship with the Father.

WEEK

3

If You Remain Silent

You and I are about to have the opportunity to test how much we believe God about who we are and the positions we hold.

1. Was Mordecai the only one in such a grief-stricken condition? If not, who were the others and exactly what did they do?

2. Why do you think Mordecai refused the change of clothes?

3. Why did Esther think Mordecai was asking too much?

4. What were the consequences of not approaching the king? What were the consequences of approaching the king? Which side seems to offer the greatest risk?

5. What special significance did the fast have that you might not have thought about?

We can protect ourselves out of our callings.

Esther 4:14

You can be brave.   _1 Cor 2:9_

Proverbs 31

Our protagonist made three shifts that moved her from self-preservation to brave determination.

how will you do it?
are you heading the direction you want to end up?
none of us are born brave

1. Esther had a **choice**.

We do get to make the choice to be courageous.

＊ "She [Esther] had to **overcome herself** in order to do what God had created her and positioned her to do."[1]

I am overcoming myself.
my biggest obstacle
God will not desert me - am I deserting Him?

You may be one brave decision from a change in your destiny.

2. Esther **faced the fear**.

There is no denial in courage. See the reality. (vs foolishness)
Most frequent command in Bible - do not be afraid.
We cherish fear.

Consider general fears, then our context's specific fear:

Everyone is overdrawn @ the moral bank.
Can you imagine living without fear?
noble character ≡ man of valor   (Proverbs 31 vs Gideon)

• Facing any **fear**

_Esther 4:16 → And if ___, then ___._
the enemy will keep using whatever we are afraid of.

And if **this**_____, then **God**.

[your answers here]

then what....?
God is faithful & good

Following Jesus - NT Wright

IF → I fear

Something is at stake that is more important than fear.

brave self preservation →
brave determination

Tony: created
cared for
crowned

Christ said, "take courage"

God offers us the courage of His presence.

Scenario #5*

It's tough being a woman in the **tight fist of fear**.

courage comes from Latin "cor" / heart.
A heart that knows it is loved.

• Facing fear of ~~death~~

destiny is way beyond the casket → all the way to the kingdom

Hebrews 2:14-15 from The Message: "By embracing death, taking it into himself, he destroyed the Devil's hold on death and freed all who **cower** through life, **scared to death of death**."

John 10:10 cannot stay in grip of fear if want to experience abundant life.

Esther 3:7 11 mos to fear

"Living perpetually in the shadow of imminent catastrophe, the Jew was threatened not only physically but psychologically. Walking in the **shadow of death** was as **plti loves** as **dying**."[2]

Are we going to die a thousand deaths fearing the 1?
Crucified with Christ — count yourself already dead.

③ Esther **took the courage** she was offered.

Gal 2:20
Col 2:13
Eph 2:6   dead in our sins
John 17:30

We are going to trade in bodies — given eternal life when saved

*Scenarios 1-4 can be found in the *Esther: It's Tough Being a Woman* Bible study.

Phil 1:6 deaths are just a part of our destiny.

Video sessions available to buy or rent at www.LifeWay.com/TheFaithful

our destiny is when Jesus returns & earth is same as heaven.

SACKCLOTH AND ASHES

"When Mordecai learned of all that had been done, he tore his clothes, put on sackcloth and ashes, and went out into the city, wailing loudly and bitterly."
ESTHER 4:1, NIV

No chapter holds greater significance to Esther than the one we're unfolding now. Today we look to the beginning of the chapter and fasten our gaze on the king's gate. Please read Esther 4:1-3.

Recall the God-ordained timing. Mordecai probably woke that morning thinking of Passover, only to discover that "he and all his Jewish friends had been sentenced to die. The rope of bondage of the exile with which he had become so comfortable had now become a noose around his neck."[3]

Reflect on Esther 4:1-3. Write two headlines that might have appeared in the next morning's newspaper, one on the front page and the other on the second, had a newspaper existed in Persia in the day of Esther.

Front Page Headline: *All Jews to be killed*

Second Page Headline: *Jews in Sackcloth & mourning*

Thus far the Book of Esther has showcased Mordecai as a very proud and capable man. Suddenly we see him wailing loudly on the public streets of Susa and tearing at his clothing.

Think of the last time you saw someone "wailing loudly and bitterly."

How did you react inside and why? *Must be really bad to not be able to control emotions*

I once sat behind a well-dressed man on an airplane who wailed until all of us around him could hardly pull ourselves together. Even if we don't know the person or share the grief, we feel an urgency to quell the demonstration—for the sufferer, but also for ourselves. Such unbridled grief reminds us of our own fragility. We see someone who has lost control and fear doing the same.

If Haman wanted a reaction from Mordecai the Jew, he certainly got one. The man's heart hemorrhaged with emotion until his skin scratched with sackcloth and his hands reddened from the rips in his garments.

PRINCIPAL QUESTION: Was Mordecai the only one in such a grief-stricken condition?

city of Susa bewildered Jews waiting...

If not, who were the others and exactly what did they do?

mourning among Jews— fasting, weeping, wailing, sackcloth; ashes

The ancients did not hide their grief. Mordecai, however, did more than stand in the streets and wail. He marched his grief straight to the king's gate so that he could be seen and heard by those with political power. In effect, he intended to make the news so that people—including the queen—would awaken to the horror of the king's edict. The place Mordecai demonstrated his mourning has an added layer of significance to him personally.

Glance back at Esther 2:19,21. Where did Mordecai work? Check one.
- ☑ At the king's gate
- ☐ At the king's gallows
- ☐ At Susa's city hall

Don't miss the fact that Mordecai took his demonstration of grief all the way to the place where he drew his paycheck. The men with whom he worked saw him at his worst and most vulnerable. Some crises are too important for saving face. Saving lives is worth losing face every time.

When was the last time you had to risk losing face to try to save something more precious than pride?

I would love to let go of pride/selfishness.

In God's economy saving is always worth losing. Now widen the lens on the city of Susa and see again the ironies that run like rivers through the Book of Esther. Within the space of two verses, Haman and King Xerxes enjoyed happy hour on one side of the gate while Mordecai wailed in sackcloth and ashes on the other. While Mordecai became the face on this picture of woe, throngs of voices joined him (see Esth. 4:3).

Lean in more closely to the Scriptures and you'll discover something even more significant about the Jews' demonstration of grief. Though the individual words appear many places in the Old Testament, the exact Hebrew phrase "with fasting, weeping, and wailing" in Esther 4:3 (NIV) appears only in Joel 2:12. Though Joel falls after Esther in our Bible, it was undoubtedly written prior to it. Many scholars believe the reference was intentional and assumed that the readers of the Book of Esther would also be familiar with the Book of Joel. I'll show you why the connection is so significant.

> Please read Joel 2:12 and fill in the space accordingly. "Even now," declares the LORD, "Return to me with all your heart, with fasting and weeping and mourning" (NIV).

Mourning is exactly the same Hebrew word translated wailing in Esther 4:3. The blanks you just filled in offer excellent insight into the actions of Mordecai and the Jews that day in Susa. They weren't just grieving. They were demonstrating their desire to do something far more proactive.

> What did Mordecai and other Jews intend to do? (Review your previous fill-in-the-blank response.)
>
> turn back to their God

Hopefully I framed the question well enough for you to see their mourning as a covenant people returning to their God. This insight could hardly be more important. From the beginning of our journey through Esther, we established that God's name may not be in the book, but it is on it. The entire theology of the book erupts from the peculiar doctrine of divine hiddenness.

One of our goals is to search for clues of God and godly activity within this most unique of sacred scrolls. You've just stumbled onto a wonderful revelation of relationship between the Jews of Susa and their God.

The reaction showed the Jews of Persia understood their peril to be associated with their wanderings from God. They had become so worldly and so thoroughly assimilated into Persian culture that they'd lost their protective shield. God had told His people from the time of Moses that He'd protect them and fight their battles for them as long as they worshiped Him only. If they forgot Him, He would still love them but He would not shield them. Instead, He'd use their enemies to turn His people back to Him.

As prophesied, God's people disobeyed Him and eventually both the Northern and Southern Kingdoms of Israel fell into captivity. Babylonian captivity ended with the decree of Cyrus, the first ruler of the Persian Empire, but the Jews in Susa and many of Persia's provinces neither regathered nor returned to Jerusalem. They remained in the comforts of a very pagan world.

When word of the edict announcing their upcoming demise hit the streets, they suddenly realized they had sinned against God and took on the actions of repentant people wishing to return. Can you grasp the great significance?

See some associations for yourself. Read Joel 2:12-17 and record every way the segment could have applied and spoken to Mordecai and the Jews strewn throughout the Persian Empire:

return to me with all your heart, with fasting, weeping, mourning rend your heart, not your garments

What do you think the phrase "rend your heart" means?

be broken, open, vulnerable ask forgiveness, confess sins

Let's target another especially rich association between the two segments. What two words are used both in Esther 4:14 and Joel 2:14?

Who knows?

The choice of words is no accident. Remember, all Scripture is God-breathed! When Mordecai framed his question to Esther with the wording "who knows," he most certainly had the words of Joel on his mind, suggesting that Esther's royal position was the means God might use to save them from calamity. *Mystery*

I learned something else very intriguing about sackcloth and ashes. Ripping off his clothes and putting on sackcloth and ashes represented a kind of public undressing and then redressing in the clothing of death to demonstrate "a change in status and state." Mordecai humbled himself "by voluntarily wearing the clothing of the poor," and "dramatically presenting himself as a dead person." The act was not only a ritual identification with the dead, but "a means of deliberately lowering one's status in the eyes of the community."[4]

[handwritten margin note: balanced with fact God loves us]

Sackcloth and ashes symbolized not only the Jews' poverty of spirit before the Lord but their complete deadness without Him. Their actions cried out, "We are dead without You, Lord! Stripped of everything! You alone can resurrect this lifeless people. Have mercy on us, Lord. We desire to return to You."

Haman succeeded in driving Mordecai to his knees after all but not in worship of a man. Instead, he drove him to return to the Lord. That, Beloved, is precisely why God allowed it. Praise Him for His infinite wisdom!

PERSONAL QUESTION: Has God ever allowed threat of trouble in your life to drive you to your knees? If so, what did you learn through the experience? *[handwritten: get out of the way]*

Of all rights bestowed on us as the children of God, perhaps none exceeds the right to repent and turn back to the Lord. I do not know where I'd be without the God-given right to repent and run back, beaten and bruised, to my God. I cannot count the times I've in effect said to Him, "I am dead without you. Destitute. Come and resurrect this lifeless woman from the grave." And He has never failed to do it. As Joel 2:13 so beautifully portrays, God is "gracious and compassionate, slow to anger and abounding in love, and he relents from sending calamity" (NIV).

[handwritten: ✳] Today's lesson is not meant to teach us to wear sackcloth and ashes and take to the public streets with our repentance; however, if that were necessary for our land's safety, many of us would humble ourselves and do it. Today's lesson is meant to teach us, in the words of the prophet Joel, to "rend [our] heart and not [our] garments" and "even now … return to [the Lord] with all [our] heart" (Joel 2:12-13, NIV).

Bask in the New Testament answer to the two-word question proposed in Joel 2:14. "Who knows?" Beloved, because of the cross of Christ Jesus, we can know. Conclude today's lesson by writing Acts 3:19-20 on a note card or piece of paper you can carry with you. Then act on it and celebrate it.

Repentance is not your punishment. It's your glorious right of daughtership. Your invitation to restoration.

"He is gracious and compassionate, slow to anger and abounding in love, and he relents from sending calamity."
JOEL 2:13, NIV

DAY 2

DEEPER THAN APPEARANCES

"When Esther's eunuchs and female attendants came and told her about Mordecai, she was in great distress. She sent clothes for him to put on instead of his sackcloth, but he would not accept them."
ESTHER 4:4, NIV

Even though I knew the story line of Esther before I ever began studying for this series, I find myself thoroughly caught up in the plot, waiting to see—and somehow even feel—what's going to happen next. An in-depth approach to Scripture changes so much. The Holy Spirit ends up unearthing hidden treasures and shedding light on details that make a narrative spring to life in a way that casual reading can't. I just love it. I also love you.

Today's Scripture segment must be painted into the same landscape as yesterday's to get the full picture. For this reason, let's begin by placing Mordecai and the Jews in the scene first, describing their appearance and actions based on Esther 4:1-3 and yesterday's lesson.

Try to describe the scene strictly from memory; then check the text to be thorough.

Mordecai in sackcloth & ashes @ city gate, wailing and refusing clothes sent by Esther. Jews afraid & realizing sin, fasting, weeping, & wailing.

As levity and aloofness twirled like ghostly dance mates on palace floors, the streets of Persia were packed with wailing Jews lying in the dirt. A pall of sackcloth blanketed the cities with such darkness that no commoner could conduct business as usual. The royals alone could exempt themselves from care.

None was more heartbroken and afraid than the one left to wonder if the lives of his people should have been worth the bending of his proud knees to Haman. "Had I only known!" Guilt is a relentless mocker even if it's misplaced. Tearing his robes and wailing bitterly, Mordecai's grief pounded on the king's gate like a battering ram.

With this backdrop vividly painted, please review Esther 4:1-3; then read verses 4-8.

Describe everything you can possibly decipher about Esther's environment based on all eight verses.

Sequestered but with "people"

Who was the obvious "go between"? *Hathach, one of king's eunuchs*

Why was he necessary?

laws

How did Esther react when she heard about Mordecai?

- tried to "quiet" him by sending clothes
- found out why
- conversation → action based on fasting ; pray

PRINCIPAL QUESTION: Why do you think Mordecai refused the change of clothes?

too important to be silenced

Our inspired narrator intended for us to feel the distance between Esther and Mordecai. Physically the two were only a gate and a walkway apart. Socially they were on different planets. We're meant to squirm under the awkwardness of Hathach's mediation and the bureaucracy that necessitated it.

The delay and relay between Esther and Mordecai doubles the drama. Together they place the scene in slow motion until we can hear the sandals of Hathach clattering down the royal halls and see the last of his robe slip through the king's gate.

We picture the eunuch trying to have a private conversation with Mordecai while thoroughly exposed in Susa's open square. Perhaps Hathach tugged on the Jew's sleeve and urged him to whisper so they would not be greatly noticed—no small feat with his charge wailing in sackcloth as he was.

Imagine what was going on in Hathach's mind as he returned to his queen with Mordecai's refusal of clothing and rebuttal of bad news. What did the eunuch have to do to memorize word-for-word the messages volleyed between them? No run-of-the-mill "he said/she said"; these were matters of state. Issues of life and death.

Picture Hathach's puzzled expressions and tense posture as he traipsed back and forth between Esther and Mordecai. Feel his rapid pulse as he pondered the prospect of relaying such highly sensitive answers. While you're at it, consider that the drama of this peculiar tête-à-tête had only just begun. It hits fever pitch tomorrow.

> Glance again at verse 4. What two groups of people told Esther about Mordecai?
> ☑ Eunuchs
> ☐ Officials
> ☑ Maids
> ☐ Stewards
> ☐ Jews

No doubt the narrator also intended to conjure a mental picture of the busy queen's quarters. We're meant to feel the frustration and irony that the one who raised Esther can hardly reach Esther. The aides buzzed around her like bees swarming their queen and probably ended up aiding her isolation more than her person. Not everyone who protects us and works hard to please helps us. Esther had become a dangerously buffered and pampered queen.

We're left to assume Esther and Mordecai rarely got to be face-to-face, and although they were clearly close to one another's hearts, for five years they had been reduced primarily to secondhand correspondence. One of the intriguing elements of the scene is how Esther—genuinely distressed—responded to the report of Mordecai's public displays of grief. Consider two ways her reactions missed the mark of Mordecai's needs and how we can relate:

ATTENTION TO APPEARANCES: Esther made no inquiry into what was wrong with Mordecai until he refused the clothes. To be fair, she may have offered him the wardrobe so he could pass through the gate and speak with her. Recall that according to 4:2, "no one clothed in sackcloth was allowed to enter" (NIV) the king's gate. Then again, several clues infer something different. We have to wonder why a change of clothes would have given Mordecai access he rarely had anyway. And if a simple switch in wardrobe would have enabled him to an audience with Esther, why on earth wouldn't he have accepted it?

Mordecai may have refused the clothes because he resented the trivial treatment for his condition. At our times of greatest crisis and chaos, who wants to be told that we'd feel better if we looked better? While we easily recognize the role of appearance in Esther's rise to position; we'd still be wise to meditate on the emotional trap she was in, especially in a culture where we are trained to share it. Changing her appearance had seemingly changed everything for Esther. Forget that she already "had a lovely figure and was beautiful" (2:7, NIV). In her experience, beauty treatments led to royal treatment.

Don't we tend to exercise the same rationale? The thought seems reasonable that our way of getting ahead should work for anyone. Esther's deep concern for Mordecai was real, but her remedy was wrong. He needed more than a change of clothes.

A change of appearance may get us through the gate, but it can't sustain us there. Sometimes we think a relationship would improve or an opportunity would arise if the person of our concern would do something about his or her lacking appearance. While a fresh haircut, neat clothes, and smaller waist may help temporarily, if the injured heart that covered itself in a sackcloth isn't treated, it will manifest its pain elsewhere. Most of our problems are a world deeper than our appearances.

> **PERSONAL QUESTION:** Think of another way we can try to help someone in crisis by, figuratively speaking, handing him or her something else to put on. Share it here.

In reality, you and I know that the favor and sovereign plan of God changed everything for Esther. Not appearances. The harem was filled with beautiful women who went through months of beauty treatments. God alone chose a Jewish orphan girl.

We've touched on Esther's attention to appearances. Now let's consider a second way she missed the mark of Mordecai's needs.

SHE ATTEMPTED A FAST FIX: Esther seemed to want to fix the problem before she even heard about it. I know the feeling. Offering a quick fix to a hurting person often can be more appealing than listening at length to the depth of his or her despair.

Simply put, sometimes we'd simply rather fix it than hear it. Why might this be true?

Our human nature not only sets us up for selfishness but to feel uncomfortable and incompetent when faced with someone who needs more than we have. Esther's situation provided the biggest set-up of all. When we consider how pampered and isolated she'd been, we may see why she prescribed a superficial dressing to a mortal wound.

If people around us helped us avoid every possible unpleasantry, fixed every hangnail, and anesthetized every headache for us, we'd quit learning how to deal with difficulty. We'd forget how to cope and we'd crush under the least inconvenience. In daily living, Beloved, strength comes from muscle, and muscle develops with a workout. This is as true spiritually as physically. What we don't use, we lose. I'd like to propose that Esther may have had "rank without substance" until now, but her life was about to change—and not because of her appearance.

Reread verse 8 carefully. List everything Mordecai told Hathach to do regarding Esther.

Notice Hathach was to do more than show the edict to Esther. He was told to explain it to her. Read her the fine print. Make sure she didn't blanket the impact with denial. Get it through her darling, crowned head. With every footfall of the eunuch to the queen's chambers, the luxury of ignorance was fleeting. Esther's superficial life was about to be shattered, and a woman much deeper than her skin was about to be unearthed. If we're blessed, the same will happen to each of us.

As painful as the process may be, that which shatters our superficiality also shatters the fetters of our fragility and frees us to walk with dignity and might to our destinies. We are not the fragile flowers we've considered ourselves to be. We, like Esther, are the warrior princesses of God.

WITHOUT BEING SUMMONED

"For any man or woman who approaches the king in the inner court without being summoned the king has but one law: that he be put to death."
ESTHER 4:11, NIV

I'm too caught up in our story line to chitchat. Let's get straight to it. Our text for today is Esther 4:9-11, but rewind to verse 6 for our reading so that we can recapture the tone. Go ahead and read the portion now. Esther 4:9 tells us that "Hathach went back and reported to Esther what Mordecai had said" (NIV).

How do you think his report entailed?

Picture Esther's face while Hathach brought the news. The moment he walked into her presence, she probably pressed anxiously, "Did you see him? Did you find out what is wrong? What is it? Tell me!" Recall that Mordecai stressed the importance to Hathach that he explain the decree to her and then express what she urgently needed to do.

Place yourself in the scene. Ask yourself some questions to experience the unfolding drama. Do you think Hathach looked the queen in the eye or looked down at the floor? What reaction do you think Esther had when Hathach mentioned Haman? Had she been suspicious of him all along? Had something about him bothered her that she couldn't put her finger on? Had she chalked it up to jealousy because he had access to the king and she didn't? Or had Haman always treated her with syrupy charm? Was she shocked by his involvement? Or did she think to herself, I knew it! I knew he was evil!

How do you imagine the scene?

How do you think Esther reacted when she learned her husband flippantly agreed to have an entire people annihilated? Think through these questions, keeping in mind that Hathach and Esther were flesh and blood. They shared our same complex emotions. A wave of fear brought swarms of butterflies to their stomachs too. Human souls are all sewn from the same fabric.

Definitive moments dot Esther. Her collision with the truth in these verses was one of them. Suddenly her crown gave her a splitting headache. As we reflected on this segment together, Melissa reminded me of a haunting similarity in *Schindler's List,* one of the most disturbing movies I've ever seen.

The film tells of German businessman Oskar Schindler, who, despite many flaws, emerged as a hero by saving the lives of over one thousand Polish Jews during the Holocaust. The villain in the movie is a Haman-figure if we'll ever see one. One of the most unsettling elements of the story was the shift back and forth between revelry and agony. One review describes how the Nazi commander had an opulent chateau looming above the labor camp. He staged parties where revelers could look down on the prisoners and watch as "the commandant randomly shoots helpless inmates as if taking target practice."[5]

Not unlike our narrative, a gate was all that stood between the sufferers and the partiers, between those in chaos and those in comfort. The movie transitions from the alarmingly detached to a man—as flawed and selfish as the rest—who could no longer resist his conscience. The obvious difference is that Esther's detachment wasn't a matter of conscience because she didn't know the travesty was underway. Her detachment came with her crown, but she'd unfortunately pulled it down around her eyes.

I wonder if, as a means of emotional survival, Esther convinced herself that what the king found valuable about her was most valuable indeed. Esther placed a high premium on appearances because they comprised her worth. She had to prioritize the superficial because it seemed to be all she had.

> When our old priorities don't go with our new life, we either return to our old life or adopt new priorities. Have you discovered this dilemma for yourself? If so, what were the circumstances?

Most critical to today's lesson, Esther had also detached from the common man's need. We tend to detach from sights and situations that make us feel bad about ourselves—especially when we feel powerless. If we think we can't do anything about a bad situation, we'd just as soon not have to see it.

Here's the trap, however: If we distance ourselves long enough from real needs, we replace them with those that aren't. Pretense becomes the new real and suddenly a delay in the delivery of our new couch becomes a terrible upset. We are wise to force ourselves to keep differentiating between simple inconveniences and authentic tribulations. The more detached and self-absorbed we become, the more we mistake annoyances for agonies. It happens to all of us.

PERSONAL QUESTION: What recent inconveniences have you been tempted to treat as if they're true tribulations?

I often have to tell myself to get a grip and downsize how I've blown up a comparatively small problem. Until now Esther's daily challenges were probably proper table settings for dignitaries and finding maids who really understood her needs. With the crisis of the Jews, however, Esther had a crisis of her own—and it was real. Through Hathach, their mediator, Mordecai had urged Esther "to go into the king's presence to beg for mercy and plead with him for her people" (v. 8, NIV).

PRINCIPAL QUESTION: Why did Esther think Mordecai was asking too much (v. 11)?

Note the hint of personal insult and injury as Esther reminded Mordecai that "all the king's officials and all the people of the royal provinces know" (NIV). In other words, "Everybody with a brain wave knows what happens if you approach the king without summons! How could you suggest such a thing?"

Mordecai had asked Esther to walk through the valley of the shadow of death. If Xerxes was tired of her and ready for a new queen, he could have used her unsolicited approach as an opportunity to take her head. No one would have questioned it. Like Vashti, the masses would have agreed that disobedient Queen Esther got what she deserved.

Esther's final statement in verse 11 is very telling. How much time had passed since Xerxes had summoned her last?

There's trouble in paradise. Apparently Esther did have a worry greater than the snag in the upholstery. Maybe five years into her marriage she feared the king's desire for her had cooled. "Whatever her fears, it seems likely that the ruthless King Xerxes will not extend the golden scepter if the queen's death would be somehow expedient to his other interests."[6]

Can you imagine having to wait to be summoned by your husband? For those of us who are married, what if, when your husband finally calls, you are commanded to drop everything and go regardless of how you feel or what you're doing? This was Esther's life. Why hadn't Xerxes called for her? Had he called for someone else instead? The Bible withholds certain answers, but we have to ask them if we're to wrestle effectively with the text.

J. G. McConville adds background to the reasons for Esther's hesitation. He explains that Persian authority demanded the inaccessibility of the king to any except those he chose to call. To infringe this etiquette was viewed as an act of treason. "To enforce the ban upon the over-bold, a squad of men armed with axes stood about the throne ready to hack them down—unless the king in his mercy extended his golden scepter to restrain them."[7]

The queen had spoken. The case was presumably closed. Hathach, surely emotionally disheveled by now, nodded his head, turned on his heels, and left the queen's quarters, bound for the wailing man in the public square.

No doubt Esther assumed that Mordecai would accept her explanation and understand the impossibility of his request. He couldn't possibly expect his beloved little Hadassah to take such a chance with her life. Or could he?

Sometimes we fear that fighting for what is right will kill us. Then again, it occurs to us that to stand by and do nothing out of self-preservation is to be dead already.

DAY 4

FOR SUCH A TIME AS THIS

"And who knows but that you have come to your royal position for such a time as this?"
ESTHER 4:14, NIV

Today we arrive at the most famous portion of the Book of Esther. If you knew only one segment of the narrative before this study, Mordecai's eloquent appeal to Esther "for such a time as this" was probably it. The segment is so vital to the narrative that we gave all of this week's video teaching to an advanced look at it.

Now we view it in context and see what other riches God has hidden there for us. Please read Esther 4:12-14. Now that we've studied the preceding verses, we've developed a more accurate picture of the awkward mediation stringing together the two-cord dialogue between Esther and Mordecai.

Name their go-between from memory, if at all possible:

When he delivered the queen's reply to Mordecai, in all likelihood both he and Esther assumed that Mordecai would concur that the risk of his request was too high. He'd see clearly that Esther could not approach the king and beg for mercy. The probability of her losing her life was too great.

To what was surely her surprise, Esther instead received such a strong and pointed response from Mordecai that we have to respect Hathach for having the courage to deliver it. Since Mordecai could not see Esther face-to-face, he intended his words to be like firm hands on her shoulders shaking the passivity out of her.

Mordecai delivered two strong points of persuasion in verses 12-14. We'll picture them as a hand on each shoulder.

Mordecai's points:

1.

2.

Let's concentrate both on what Mordecai said and implied. Notice he stated the negative implication of inaction followed by the positive implication of action. Look first at the negative implication. In Esther 4:13 Mordecai shook her with the risk she hadn't considered. "In case you've forgotten, you are Jewish too. If you do nothing, you and your father's family will perish."

David A. Clines says this was not so much a threat as the other pan of the balance in which Esther's fate was being weighed. Ironically staying out of the king's presence was no less dangerous than entering it—an irony Vashti had already encountered. "One queen stays out when bidden, the other will enter when unbidden; but whereas Vashti risked only the wrath of the king, Esther risks the king's sentence of death or else a divine punishment on her and her family."[8]

Circle the phrase "the other pan of the balance."

Here's a graphic of the implied scale. I've purposely displayed it in perfect balance. Here's how I'd like you to view it: Up until verse 13, Esther had only weighed the consequences of approaching the king. She'd not considered the consequences of refusing.

PRINCIPAL QUESTION: Please "weigh" both risks by describing them on each side of the scale.

APPROACHING   REFUSING

Now that you see the risks on both sides, which seems weightier? On the side of the risk that weighs most, draw an arrow down. On the side of the risk that weighs less, draw an arrow up.

After Mordecai shook Esther by one shoulder, he grabbed her by the other. This time he stressed the positive implication of action: "Esther, what if you were born for this very moment? Think how unlikely your position is! What about all the events that led to your queenship! Why on earth did we stay here and not go to Jerusalem when we could? Why was Vashti deposed? Why were you the exact right age at the exact right time to be chosen for the harem?

"Why, amid so many girls, were the eunuchs so partial to you? Why did they go out of their way to help you? More astonishingly, why did the king have such favor on you? Why didn't he just make you one of his concubines? What in the world made him marry you and set the crown on your head? Hadassah! Open your eyes! Why is a Jewish woman the Queen of Persia at such a time as this? Must it not be providence? Must it not be God?"

We see God's providence in Esther's life because her position held such importance, but perhaps you're having trouble relating this to your life. At first, I did too. We may think Mordecai's exhortation to Esther has little relevance to us. How much do we really have in common? For starters, we're not queens, nor do many of us hold the kinds of high positions that invite an obvious parallel. Furthermore, we can't imagine the fulfillment of one comparatively insignificant destiny affecting so much or so many.

You and I are about to have the opportunity to test how much we believe God about who we are and the positions we hold.

> **PERSONAL QUESTION:** Look up the following Scriptures and record what they say about you and your position if you are a follower of Jesus Christ. With each then candidly circle how you tend to apply each segment by choosing one of the four descriptions: Figuratively, spiritually, literally, or I don't apply it at all. (By "spiritually" I mean the tendency to limit the application to a spiritualization that is somehow true in God-terms but not in "real" terms. The exercise will be most helpful if you're painfully honest.)
>
> **MATTHEW 11:11**
> I tend to apply this Scripture ...
> Figuratively   Spiritually   Literally   Not at all
>
> **MATTHEW 13:11-12**
> I tend to apply this Scripture ...
> Figuratively   Spiritually   Literally   Not at all
>
> **LUKE 17:20-21**
> I tend to apply this Scripture ...
> Figuratively   Spiritually   Literally   Not at all

1 CORINTHIANS 4:20
I tend to apply this Scripture ...
Figuratively   Spiritually   Literally   Not at all

1 PETER 2:9
I tend to apply this Scripture ...
Figuratively   Spiritually   Literally   Not at all

REVELATION 1:6
I tend to apply this Scripture ...
Figuratively   Spiritually   Literally   Not at all

REVELATION 5:9-10
I tend to apply this Scripture ...
Figuratively   Spiritually   Literally   Not at all

Beloved, absorb this with your whole heart: You are royalty. Not figurative royalty. Not just spiritual royalty. You are in the most literal sense possible the daughter of the universe's King. You have royal blood in a way that even Esther did not. The crimson bloodline of Christ flows through your veins.

For now the kingdom of God on this earth resides within you, but one day your eyes will spring open to the most brilliant reality sight can behold. The kingdom of God will surround you, complete with palace, mansions, streets, and horses. In ways incomprehensible now, you will reign there with Him. All that we now call "reality" will be a mere shadow of the vivid world we have coming. Right now you are representing the King on official business in another land, but you are no less royal than the Queen of England would be if she visited the White House. Or the Bronx. She is queen regardless of where she is and how she is treated. Her status is secure. So is yours. When she's cut, she bleeds royal blood. So do you.

Not only are you royalty but you also have been placed in your sphere of influence, regardless of the size you perceive it to be, "for such a time as this." Ecclesiastes 3:2 tells us there is "a time to be born and a time to die" (NIV). God cut out those exact perimeters for you and me on the kingdom calendar so that we would be positioned on earth right now. Likewise, Acts 17:26 tells us unflinchingly that God "marked out [our] appointed times in history and the boundaries of [our] lands" (NIV). You see, even your current location is part of the set-up for your kingdom destiny. In Christ "we were also chosen, having been predestined according to the plan of him who works everything in conformity with the purpose of his will" (Eph. 1:11, NIV). These realizations should be stunning and marvelous to us, exploding our lives with significance.

The hard truth of Mordecai's exhortation to Esther also applies to us. We can refuse to walk in obedience to God or cower in fear from our calling and He will undoubtedly still accomplish His agenda. As for us, however, we will pass up the fulfillment of our own entire life-purpose and we—and perhaps even "our father's family"—will miss a mighty work. Frighteningly, perhaps even a mighty deliverance. One of our biggest obstacles in our most important moments "for such a time as this" is the difficulty of the destiny-serving task.

Know the feeling? So do I. Every giant-size weight drops into our laps right on schedule. None of our purposes will be fulfilled easily. All of them will require the most difficult decisions we think we can make. Decisions that we may feel will practically kill us. Then God does something miraculous and we become something we're not. That's when "who knows?" becomes "I know."

At some of the hardest times in my life, I have been able to make the more difficult choice out of pure blind-eyed, bent-kneed acceptance that it was somehow part of a greater plan. I was beaten by a conviction that throbbed relentlessly against my strong self-centeredness. As much as my flesh wanted relief, I knew that when all was said and done, I'd sit on that side of glory having much rather fulfilled my calling than served myself all the way to meaninglessness. I had to accept that I was not called to an easy life. I was called to a purposeful life.

Are you coming to some of the same conclusions? If so, what circumstances have helped you?

At strategic times of internal war I stop and ask myself, "What if this is a critical moment? What if this very thing, this very decision, is the most important piece of the puzzle comprising my purpose?"

God has profoundly used the conviction that those heightened times of decision in my toughest trials could be "make it or break it" moments in my destiny. Much like Mordecai suggested, I always knew God would accomplish His will and do what He intended, but if I made a man-ward (vs. God-ward) decision, I'd be left out of a divine loop that would eventually mean everything to me.

Beloved, in the times of greatest struggle when you make the God-ward decision over convenience, earthly comfort, or carnal pleasure, you too have come to a critical moment in the fulfillment of your destiny. A defining moment. A war is being waged over your head in the unseen realm, and a great cloud of witnesses is cheering you on. You have no idea what's at stake.

FAST FOR ME

"Fast for me. Do not eat or drink for three days, night or day. I and my attendants will fast as you do."
ESTHER 4:16, NIV

Recently I've felt drawn once again to the long-winded acrostic sprawled across the pages of Psalm 119. I love its unbridled celebration of the Word. Verses 92 and 93 are among my favorites: "If your law had not been my delight, I would have perished in my affliction. I will never forget your precepts, for by them you have preserved my life" (NIV).

In Melissa's old vernacular of "Amen," *true that.* Without the Word of God as my daily bread, I would honestly be buried in a pit so deep that I wouldn't recognize daylight.

I also love verse 37. "Turn my eyes away from worthless things; preserve my life according to your word" (NIV). God has used the fascination He's placed in my heart for Scripture to turn my eyes from so many worthless things. The store shelves are filled with books, magazines, and movies that reinforce a warped worldview. They make you unhappy with monogamy and even unhappier with yourself in ways you cannot fix.

Many people who know how neck-deep you and I are in Bible study don't understand our affinity for it. They still picture Scripture reading like taking a beating or like swallowing a dose of terrible-tasting medicine to get over a virus. They have no idea that it just may give you one instead.

Until they get into Bible study for themselves, they can't imagine how thrilling it can be and how healthy and free their minds can feel. Think about this for a moment: Many of the women in our small-group Bible studies today tried a taste of it because they saw your joy and the impact it had on you. Praise God, a voracious love for His Word is gloriously contagious! Agree with me in prayer this moment that more and more women will catch this holy virus and never get over it.

Please read Esther 4:15-17.

What exhortation had Mordecai sent through Hathach to Esther in the previous verses (4:13-14)?

Based on the verses you've just read, how influential was his plea?

What had Esther decided to do?

Even though Esther would approach the king alone, she had no intention of preparing alone.

What did Esther call for?

What kind of fast was it?

What groups of people or individuals were told to participate in the fast?

The fast Esther commissioned holds chief significance for several reasons:

THE CONTRAST: The most pronounced motif in the entire Book of Esther is feasting. The chapters are practically tied together by tablecloths. Not coincidentally, this fast divides the feasts in the narrative in half, strongly implying that the remaining feasts only occur because this fast took place.

THE TIMING: Remember, the news of the decree hit the provinces the very day the Passover celebration was intended to begin among the Jews. Feasting was the cornerstone of the entire remembrance. Only something monumental could have trumped the commanded ritual, turning its feasting into fasting. Perhaps we can best relate by imagining dreadful news on Christmas Day, calling for fasting while turkeys roast in the oven and pies cool on kitchen counters. The emotional whiplash would be brutal.

THE SEVERITY: In the ancient world most fasts were either limited to daylight hours or certain foods and rarely included fasting from water. The risk of dehydration was too serious. Severe maladies often call for severe remedies, however. Perhaps most interesting is what this kind of fast would do to Esther's appearance. Remember, the harem girls were fattened up for the king, not starved into sticks.

THE IMPLICATION: A momentous element of the fast in Esther is the profound implication of prayer. In a book of the Bible with no mention of God, fasting indicates prayer. And prayer indicates God. After all, fasting for fasting's sake is futile. Our assumption is that Esther and the Jews of Susa went without food so they could wholeheartedly focus their petitions before God. Their refusal to receive sustenance demonstrated their desperation to receive something much greater: deliverance.

> PRINCIPAL QUESTION: Glance back at all four of the reasons why the fast held special significance. Name one among them that you might not have thought about and explain why.

> On day 1 of this week's study we compared the scene of mourning, sackcloth, and ashes at the opening of chapter 4 with the words of Joel 2:12-17. Fill in the following blanks according to verses 15-16.
> "Blow the _____ in Zion, _____ a
> holy _____, call a sacred assembly. _____ the
> _____" (NIV).

> List every way these verses parallel Esther's actions in Esther 4:15-16.

In the whole of Israel's history, God's people were never called to fast for fasting's sake. They were called to forego food to deny all else but God. We must ask ourselves why this occasion would be any different. The following portion of Joel 2:17 describes a petition God's people were told to make as they gathered together for a holy fast: "Let them say, 'Spare your people, O LORD. Do not make your inheritance an object of scorn, a byword among the nations'" (NIV).

How closely would you say this petition echoes the one the Jews in Susa needed to make?

The parallels in Esther 4:15-17 could not be more remarkable. Perhaps they find the height of their significance in the way they etch "God" in the blanks of this unique book. Consider the words of Dr. Karen Jobes:

> "Whether Esther was mindful of Joel's prophecy or not, she in effect 'blows the trumpet in Zion,' commanding Mordecai to call a fast for all the Jews of Susa, to see if the Lord may relent from sending this calamity on her people. For the first time in this story Esther identifies herself with God's people and responds to the prophetic call to repentance by joining with the Jews of Susa in this fast."[9]

I love the imagery Dr. Jobes assigns to Esther as one blowing the trumpet. Who was less likely? We simply have no idea what God will do with even the most reluctant life. Some leap to their destinies. Others lag and loom, yet God persists, "for God's gifts and his call are irrevocable" (Rom. 11:29, NIV).

The very woman who had hidden her identity so she could live royally in Persia stood to her feet and blew the trumpet of regathering loudly for the scattered people of Zion. The shrill sound reverberated from palace walls to peasant homes until thousands of voices melded together in heavenly ascension: "Spare Your people, O LORD!" A splintered people became as one timber. She who had systematically reinvented herself returned to her roots at the risk that she'd be buried by them.

Esther came to what many would call her "defining moment." Sometimes our most important moments come hand-in-hand with our willingness to reveal that we aren't really who we've seemed to be. Our protagonist was a double-minded woman who, interestingly enough, possessed a name for each side of herself. She was Hadassah, the Jewess, and Esther, the Persian. I can't imagine that any of us has persistently resisted the lure of double-mindedness.

What two names might represent your duplicity?

_____ the _____

_____ the _____

I struggled terribly in my adolescence and young adulthood with desires to be both smart and gullible. Both innocent (which I felt I'd never been) and alluring (which I felt was all I could hope to be). Both godly and deadly. Then God allowed hardship and consequence to press against me from both sides until a decision had to be made and part of me had to die. Consider these words describing Esther's dilemma and, in turn, our own: "In a crisis situation such as this, there was no neutral position. Failure to decide brings personal loss and misses the opportunity to fulfill God's purposes."[10]

PERSONAL QUESTION: Circle "failure to decide." What do those words convey to you personally?

At times nothing is more consequentially decisive than refusing to make a decision. At critical moments—even those unrecognizable at the time—failure to decide is to decide on failure. As a warring concoction of anxiety and hunger overtook her, Esther wrestled until one part of her, wounded and weary, won. She was a Jew and, ironically, her exposure would prove her a poor one. She'd mustered every ounce of her strength to side with her weakness. Though the pious and pagan alike might think her a failure, she'd not be guilty of a failure to decide.

Esther would identify herself with her covenant people even if it killed her. If it didn't, life as she'd known it was dead anyway. There was no way back. She must step into the unknown known and into the hiddenness completely unhidden.

Fully exposed, only a providential force could protect her now. Xerxes' scepter was in the hand of God.

Hosea

Hosea displayed faithfulness on multiple levels. He faced an unusual and difficult assignment from God. He was to demonstrate God's faithfulness to an unfaithful people through marriage to an unfaithful woman. What a calling! Hosea obeyed, proving faithfulness to both God and Gomer, his wife.

Hosea served in the Northern Kingdom of Israel as a prophet in the eighth century B.C. Most scholars think it was around the time between 760 and 720 B.C. He most likely ministered for about forty years before the Northern Kingdom was conquered by Assyria. His ministry came at a critical time for the nation which was at peace and prosperous, but spiritually bankrupt.

In the first chapter of the Book of Hosea, God told the prophet to marry "a woman of promiscuity and have children of promiscuity" (1:2). Hosea invited such pain into his life to represent the pain God experienced as Israel, His wife (see 2:16), had been selling herself to other gods and abandoning worship of the Lord.

Throughout the book, we see Hosea return to Gomer again and again, seeking to restore her, and remaining faithful to his wife even as she was unfaithful to him. In this picture, we see our faithful God, redeeming us, remaining faithful even when we are not.

This week's study begins in the middle of the action of the book. Hosea has taken Gomer as his wife and she has had three children, with names meaning God Shows, No Compassion, and Not My People. Gomer then returns to her promiscuity.

Hosea later goes back to his wife and that is where this week picks up.

Through the story of Hosea, Gomer, and their tragically named children, God demonstrates His neverending love for His people. All throughout the Bible, God displays His compassion. God calls His children "My people." He loves with a steadfast love, redeeming our unfaithfulness and restoring our hope.

The faithfulness we have or see in these heroes of the Bible merely reflects the ultimate faithfulness of our steadfast God. The story of Hosea teaches us how much our God loves us, His people.

ABOUT HOSEA: UNFAILING LOVE CHANGES EVERYTHING

Originally published in 2015, *Hosea: Unfailing Love Changes Everything* is a 7-session women's Bible study written by Jennifer Rothschild. Through this study, you'll be guided to understand, but more especially to apply, the message of the prophet of love.

ABOUT JENNIFER ROTHSCHILD

Known for her substance and a down-to-earth style, Jennifer Rothschild weaves together colorful illustrations, universal principles, and music to help audiences find contentment, walk with endurance, and celebrate the ordinary. Through wit and poignant storytelling, Jennifer relates challenges in her life that prompt women to look beyond their circumstances to find unique gifts in unusual packaging.

WEEK

4

Loved Again

Gomer tried to find identity
in herself and lovers because
she never identified with
her new identity as a
chosen, loved woman.

VIEWER GUIDE

destroyed

WHEN YOU AIN'T GOT YADA, YOU AIN'T GOT NADA

When we wander from God, usually our problem is a lack of **Knowledge.**

Hosea 4:6

When we see the word *know* in the Book of Hosea, it is usually the Hebrew word *yada* which means "an **intimate** knowing."

vs information

When we stray from God, we stray from our sense of self because we don't yada our **source** of self.

Sarah did not **value** herself because she did not yada God.

her source of s

Ruth
Call me
"Mara"
bitterness

Naomi's grandson, Obed, grew up to become the father of Jesse and Jesse the father of **David**. And Jesus Christ came from the **lineage** of David.

Hosea 6:6

In the Book of Hosea, "knowledge of God" is *daath Elohim* in Hebrew and shows an empathetic **connection** to God. *an awareness of how God fee*

lost their first love

Revelation 2:5 gives us the following steps to yada:

1. Consider from where you have **fallen**.

2. **Repent**. *change thinking*

3. Do the things you did at **first**.

God doesn't want us to sacrifice **relationship** with Him for activity for Him.

spiritual apathy / wandering
root: hard hearts w/o experience of God

Intimacy with Jesus

to know God is to love God

straying from God is symptom not problem
Gomer = Israel = us

loyal love
knowledge of God vs burnt offerings

let us press on to knowledge of God   HOSEA 6

Hosea 2   ~~both~~ betroth you
Psalm 63   active knowing

God's Word equips us to know Him

Experience Jesus
Be the beloved

don't sacrifice relationship for activity

if Gomer had known her value and Hosea,
she wouldn't have strayed

THE BUY BACK

Then the LORD said to me, "Go again; show love to a woman who is loved by another man and is an adulteress, just as the LORD loves the Israelites though they turn to other gods and love raisin cakes."
HOSEA 3:1, HCSB

Hey, you loved, accepted, and complete woman of God! You, Gomer Girl, are the beloved!

This week we are going to experience incredible forgiveness and restoration. So, let's go back to the slave block where we left Gomer, hopeless and alone. That is a terrible way to leave a friend, isn't it? And I feel like Gomer is a friend. Do you? Even though we left her alone on the slave block, she was not forgotten. While Gomer was feeling unloved, God and Hosea had something totally radical in mind.

Look at Hosea 3:1 again. What did God tell Hosea to show?

Notice what God did not tell Hosea to do. God didn't say, "Go show judgment" or "Go show disdain to your wife." God told Hosea to show love. Love! Gomer had not only been loved by "another" (that may have been a ginormous understatement), she had likely been loved by many others.

We've been trying to identify with Gomer, but shift for a second. How would you feel if you were Hosea, asked to do such a thing?

He must have felt betrayed, like it wasn't fair, or right, that he should have to do such a thing. It had to be incredibly humbling.

At that moment, maybe Hosea needed to love God more than he loved Gomer in order to obey. We can't forget that Hosea was not super-husband. He was human-husband. He had to feel hurt by Gomer. He probably fought feelings of disgust. He was certainly humiliated in front of the men in town. He was a spiritual leader in the community, and his wife had left him and committed flat-out, in-your-face adultery, over, and over.

We cannot overestimate what this must have been like for him and how he must have felt. But he was called by God and he followed God. I can only imagine that His willingness to obey gave him the strength to obey. And deep down, don't you hope he still loved her? Missed her? Either way, it took sheer humility and strength to go get her back.

But he went.

According to Hosea 3:2, what was the payment he gave for her?

He paid fifteen shekels of silver, a homer of barley, and a lethech of barley (ESV). Well, I don't know about you, but that was totally meaningless to me. I had no idea what value that represented in their time. So I looked it up.

In verse 2 the use of the word *lethech* is a *hapax legomenon*. What? You don't know what that is? Ha! I sure didn't. *Hapax legomenon* means a word which occurs only once in a document. *Lethech* appears in the Old Testament only here in Hosea 3:2.

Because of this unique use of the word in Hosea, the versions differ on the translation of verse 2. Some translators assume that the lethech is a half of a homer. Yeah, that means a lot to you, I know. So here's the straight scoop on a homer. It was a unit of dry measure, estimated between 3.8 and 6.6 bushels. Others assume that the homer and the lethech are different terms for dry measures, but, that too, makes me scratch my head and say, "huh?" Some versions even render that word as a skin of wine. After reading all of the educated guesses, I have to go with the idea that the lethech was likely a half a homer.

Likely, a homer and a half of barley was worth about fifteen pieces of silver. So if you do the math, Gomer has a price tag on her of thirty pieces of silver. So picture it—fifteen pieces of silver and a big ole bag of barley along with a not-so-big bag of barley. That's what it cost Hosea to get Gomer back. Next let's try to get a grip on how valuable Gomer was.

According to Exodus 21:32, what was valued at thirty pieces of silver?

Gomer was equal in value to a slave according to the law of the goring ox in Exodus. Now, look at Leviticus 27:2-4. What else was valued at thirty shekels of silver?

In Leviticus 27:2, the NIV renders the idea of making a vow to dedicate someone to the Lord. If you were dedicating a woman, you were to be assessed thirty pieces of silver. The NASB translation reads when you make a "difficult vow" you are to be charged based on the value of the person. It's kind of like how an insurance company would pay more for an injury based on time lost from work.

So put yourself on the slave block with Gomer. How much would you hope someone would pay for you if that price suggested your value?

What does the truth of 1 Peter 1:18-19 suggest about your value?

You were worth the life of Jesus. That is how valuable you are to Him. You may not feel that special or valuable, but, Gomer Girl, who you are and how you feel are not the same thing. Trust God's opinion of you. He sees you as incredibly, eternally, valuable.

What are your thoughts? Formulate them into a prayer of thanks to God, or a prayer of petition asking God to help you internalize the truth of your value.

Back to the slave block. Hosea paid thirty pieces of silver for Gomer—the price of a slave. What if you were purchased with the cost of a slave? How would you expect to be treated?

I would expect to be a lifelong slave of the one who bought me.

When Hosea spoke to Gomer after redeeming her, he didn't say, "Come home and serve me. Be my slave." He could have, right? After all, he just bought her for the price of a slave.

But Hosea 3:3 doesn't give that impression.

What does Hosea invite Gomer to do in Hosea 3:3?

He asks her to live with him as his wife in faithfulness. He tells her there will be a short time of probation, and he will be faithful to her too. But he does not say that her role is forever altered. No more wife, now just the house keeper. No more wife, now just the concubine. The beauty of her redemption is that it includes restoration.

So does your redemption. It includes restoration.

What was lost in the garden was redeemed on the cross. What sin destroyed in Eden, God restored through Calvary!

Oh, sister! I feel a verse coming on! You need to find 2 Corinthians 5:17, change the word "he" to "she" and read it out loud now. Right now. Yes, now! Louder!

If you are in Christ, my fellow Gomer, old things are passed away and behold! That means, stop and notice! Behold, poof! All, not just some, but all, all things are made new! Redeemed and restored! Thank You, Jesus!

God does not redeem without restoring. Even Israel will be restored to the bride again. Eugene Peterson paraphrases God's restorative words to Israel this way: "Never again will you address me, 'My slave-master!'" (Hosea 2:16, The Message).

When God redeems us—even though we may feel like we have no valuable position in His heart; even though we may feel like a slave—God expects us to treat Him not as slave-master but as husband. That means we must receive our identity as the loved, accepted bride and act like it. We must trust in His love and forgiveness.

Finally, for today, I want you to think about thirty pieces of silver. That phrase sounds familiar doesn't it?

> What New Testament reference to thirty pieces of silver comes to mind? If you want to check, look to Matthew 26:15. Who was also sold for that price?

> How does it make you feel that Jesus allowed Himself to be sold for the price of a slave? How does it make you feel that Jesus specifically connected His value to that of a woman? Write your feelings to Him.

Oh Gomer Girl, He made Himself nothing so we could be somebody. His beautiful life gives our lives beauty. Let's honor Him with our humility and gratefulness today. Amen!

GOD'S SHOCKING RESPONSE

Therefore, I am going to persuade her,
lead her to the wilderness,
and speak tenderly to her.
HOSEA 2:14, HCSB

Let's summarize where we are in Hosea. Both Israel and Gomer have followed crooked paths straight into trouble! They have chased after other lovers. They have betrayed the one who loved them most.

We can't fully identify with how God must have felt, but have you ever felt betrayed? How did you feel?

Betrayal makes me feel unimportant, hurt, dishonored, and angry. When I have felt betrayed, I want to run as far from that person as possible and never trust them again. In my not-so-Christlike moments, I want them to feel as awful as they made me feel. Punish the rascal!

I'm an imperfect woman, and my response is imperfect too.

But how would you expect a perfect God to respond?
☐ destroy them
☐ remove His blessing from them
☐ ignore them
☐ punish them
☐ other

God has every right to rebuke and destroy. If you want to see what I mean, read Hosea 10:2.

God would be just in His actions if He destroyed them down to the subatomic level. But He doesn't. Instead of speaking harshly, the long-suffering God of Israel speaks tenderly to His people.

Is that not almost too much to bear? Just when you think God is done, He does not treat any of us as our sins deserve. In fact, He shows us kindness.

Look at Romans 2:4 and jot down the result of God's kindness.

I will go back to my former husband,
for then it was better for me than now.
HOSEA 2:7, HCSB

What does Hosea 2:7 reveal about God's hopeful expectation?

God treats His people kindly and holds out hope that Israel will repent and return to the truth that God alone is the perfect Lover of their souls.

But look at Hosea 2:15. God wants us to return because He wants to bless us.

Fill in the blanks to reveal the blessing.

There I will _____ and

make the Valley of Achor into a _____ of_____ (HCSB).

God's going to make her valley of trouble into a door of hope! Have you heard of the Valley of Achor?

When the Israelites, under the leadership of Joshua, entered the promised land, one of the first places they came upon was a valley near Jericho. The valley was called Achor. The word *Achor* means *muddy* or *turbid*. The name may be connected to the rolling waters of the Jordan at flood stage. So here's how to view the Valley of Achor:

1. THE EARLY DAYS

When Israelite grandmas were kneading dough and talking about the good old days when they first lived in their homeland, they would have thought of Achor. It would be like the early days in some phase of your life. Maybe it was when you moved into your first apartment, or when you went away to college. If you've been married a while, you can think of some images that represent being newlywed, right? I still have my first $35 wedding band that Phil gave me when I said "I do." It was all we could afford, and when I think of our early days, I think of that ring. You know, like that ugly green couch you got at a garage sale. Or, perhaps the image that comes to mind when you think of your freshman year of college are the stuffed peppers that were served every Thursday in the cafeteria.

Those images would be like the Israelites' remembrance of the churning Jordan at flood stage. Think of it like nostalgia—fond memories even if everything wasn't always perfect. These are the sweet memories that conjure up remembrances of the early days—the good old days.

> What image comes to your mind when you think of the early days of some special phase of life for you?

My $35 wedding band and what you wrote above are the sweet images of your Valley of Achor. But it isn't always sweet memories associated with the early days; sometimes it's bittersweet to remember your own "Valley of Achor."

2. THE HARD DAYS

The Valley of Achor was also bittersweet to the Israelites. Look at Joshua 7 if you need to recount how Israel conquered Jericho. It was a big city—a big victory. They had sweet memories of their first steps into the promised land. Then, they attacked Ai. It was a little city, but a big loss. This was a bitter memory for Israel because Achan's disobedience was the reason they lost to Ai. Achan and his family were then stoned—in the Valley of Achor. So, the image of Achor not only evoked the early days for Israel, but also a particular time of defeat and shame.

> Do you have some Valley of Achor memories that are painful to think about?

The wonderful times can also host the worst times. When I think of early days of my marriage, I can't help but think of that cheap wedding band and smile. But I can also think of some ugly fights Phil and I had as newlyweds trying to adjust to married life—those Achor moments don't make me smile at all.

Get the point of Achor? Taken together I think the Valley of Achor represented promise followed by problems. Triumph followed by trouble.

It's the human story, isn't it? Sterling silver shines and then tarnishes. Gomer says, "I do" and then says, "What have I done?" We walk in faith and then we wander off into unfaithfulness.

You can even see this in our American story. The early days of JFK's presidency were like Camelot, but it quickly turned into Achor when he was assassinated. Make sense?

Wayward Israel, and hopeless Gomer, would have heard this and it was as if God was saying, "I'll take the lowest point in your life, the time of spoiled potential, dashed hopes, and greatest shame, and I'll turn that into a honeymoon of new beginnings."

Wow. What a God!

Do you need God to turn your Valley of Achor into a door of hope? Oh Gomer Girl, He can and He wants to.

Write a prayer asking Him to open that door of hope, to be the door of hope you need.

We Gomer Girls need each other. Find a Bible Study buddy you can invite into your Valley of Achor. She can help that valley of trouble become a door of hope as she shines the light of Jesus over painful memories.

Jesus Himself is your Door of Hope, sweet Gomer Girl. He loves, accepts, and completes you. So walk in His rest and restoration today.

BACK TO THE DAYS OF OUR YOUTH

And she will sing there as in the days of her youth,
As in the day when she came up from the land of Egypt.
HOSEA 2:15b, NASB

I tell you, sister, the older I get, the more forgetful I get! Can I get a witness? Well, I found out why. When you and I were born, we came with all the brain cells we will ever get. That's why when you were a newborn, your head was one-quarter of your total length at birth. All those valuable brain cells don't regenerate once they're gone. So once those sweet little cells are damaged, they are not replaced. That is why your brain is reduced to only one-eighth of your total length by the time you reach adulthood. Sometimes I would love to have my brain restored to the proportion it was when I was in diapers!

Look at the second half of Hosea 2:15 and jot down what God promises about Israel's youth.

If your brain cells are behaving today, think about your youth. What was the very best part of youth for you?

One of Israel's best memories had to be when God delivered them from slavery in Egypt.

I imagine they came out singing. But, shortly after, they were singing the blues, wandering in wilderness, disobeying God, losing battles, and worshiping idols. Sour notes for sure.

God is saying, "I am not only going to redeem you now, but my redemptive touch will not be confined to the present or even to the future." God's work in our lives renews everything that has come before—our best days and our worst days.

Let's visit another prophet, Joel, to see how this redemption and renewal works. He used a locust plague in the same way Hosea used his marriage as a sermon illustration. (Not to suggest a marriage partner and locusts have anything in common. *Wink!*)

What does Joel 2:25 promise to the ancient Israelites?

Just as none of us are as young as we once were, all of us have places in our lives where the "locusts" have eaten—hopes dashed, mistakes made, and losses piled on. God says He will repay all that damage.

What do you think God means when He says He will repay? (Attention Type A: there is no right answer; I just want you to think about this.)

The word *repay* in Joel 2:25 is *shalam*. Sound familiar? What word comes to mind when you see *shalam*? I bet you'd say peace. Me too; that's what comes to mind. But this word *shalam* means "to be safe (in mind, body or estate); figuratively, to be (causatively, make) completed."

Since Joel was talking about damage done in the past, he promised two things. God will make us safe from past damage, and He will make it somehow complete.

When Gomer said "I do" to Hosea, she became the beloved bride—complete. Her past was overwritten by her present. And, then, when she strayed and became enslaved, Hosea redeemed her and made her safe—even from past damage.

The idea that God completes our past, helps me understand Romans 8:28 even better. It says God makes all things work for the good of those who love Him, right?

How does Joel's promise to make past damage both safe and complete add to your understanding or appreciation of Romans 8:28?

God works all things together, including my past damage, for good. How?

Sweet Gomer Girl, you may have endured something so awful in your past that you can't even imagine God redeeming it and restoring shalam to you. But His promise is true. What the Enemy stole, God will *shalam*. What selfish people have taken from you, God will repay.

Faithful Job went through so much loss, but the worst of it had to be the loss of his children. You know his story, right? Well, after so much damage, Scripture says, "the LORD blessed the last part of Job's life more than the first… He also had seven sons and three daughters" (Job 42:12-13, HCSB). I think it is wonderful of God to shalam all Job's loss, but, seven new sons and three new daughters do not replace the children Job lost. They were an added blessing, but not a replacement. At least that's the way my mom heart feels.

I think all parents know that replacing a lost child with other children is impossible. Though a parent loves the new child like crazy, the hole in our heart from the lost child is still there. Yet the message of Job suggests God has restored all of Job's losses. Could Joel 2:25 and Hosea 2:15b speak to the same mystery?

Hosea says God will restore Gomer/Israel so they will respond as they did in their youth. Joel promises God will repay what has been taken away, making it both safe and complete. Paul says all things work for our good. Job was blessed beyond all he had lost.

Write down your thoughts and observations about what these four Scriptures have in common.

God may not replace what you have lost, but He will repay what you have lost. He will shalam. Look at Genesis 50:20 and speak that truth to your past damage and loss. Seriously, sister. You may even need to stand up, turn around as if you are addressing your past, and quote that truth to it.

You intended to harm me, but God intended it for good to accomplish what is now being done…
GENESIS 50:20, NIV

Good job! I am cheering you on and saying it right along with you.

Gomer Girl, you are not your past! You are not what has happened to you. You are not your struggle. You are not someone else's opinion. You are not your fear or insecurity. You are loved, accepted, and complete. You are the beloved.

So, you tell your past that it is not the boss of you. God will *shalam*—He literally will help you make peace with your past.

In my favorite C. S. Lewis book, *The Great Divorce*, the author has an imaginary conversation with one of his heroes, George MacDonald, as they sit together just outside of Heaven. MacDonald tells Lewis; "'Son,' he said, 'ye cannot in your present state understand eternity ... That is what mortals misunderstand. They say of some temporal suffering, "No future bliss can make up for it," not knowing that Heaven, once attained, will work backwards and turn even that agony into a glory.'"[1]

What he's saying is that even your most agonizing loss, even your worst day, will be cast in the light of shalam—redeemed and restored as all things are made new.

> Finish today by reading Hosea 6:1-3. Of what worst day and best day do those days make you think?

The "two days" and "the third day" are Hosea shouting into the future that "the Door of Hope" will swing wide open for all mankind to walk through. Jesus' death and resurrection redeem, renew, restore, and revive us!

The resurrection of Jesus reminds us that the worst day is not the last day.

"In the third day he will raise us up and we shall live in his sight" (KJV). Dear one, that literally means, "We will live before His face." And there we will stand in purity and sing as in the days of our youth.

> But I trust in your unfailing love; my heart rejoices in your salvation.
> I will sing the Lord's praise, for he has been good to me.
> **PSALM 13:5-6, NIV**

MY WIFE IN RIGHTEOUSNESS

> I will take you to be My wife forever.
> I will take you to be My wife in righteousness,
> justice, love, and compassion.
> **HOSEA 2:19, HCSB**

I've been thinking about you and praying for you as you read Hosea's words. I am trusting God's Word to be comfort and life to you. If you are broken, I am trusting God to bind your wounds with His beautiful, healing Word. Though I cannot really explain how, I believe God's restoration is so complete that it redeems the past as well as the present and future. I need that kind of redemption, especially in the areas where I feel like such a mess!

I think we all have those times or areas in our lives when we feel like a mess, right?

Let's pick up in Hosea 2:19 and see what we are to God. At this point, you don't even need to read the verse to answer this question, but here it goes anyway…

To whom does God compare us in this verse?

Note the description of God's commitment. He takes us to be His wife forever in: _____, _____, _____ and _____.

Right next to each word, write how that quality responds to sin.

Righteousness:

Love:

Justice:

Compassion:

Did you notice how those four words put together represent the perfect balance in a relationship? That is how God relates to us, with perfect balance.

Righteousness and justice point fingers of guilt and mandate sin be punished. Love and compassion cover guilt and forgive sin. Righteousness and love complete each other; justice and compassion balance each other.

Those four words describe the nature of God's covenant to you. How do you expect Him to treat you most often? With righteousness and justice, or love and compassion?

The right answer technically is "yes!" In other words, a perfect God who loves perfectly will relate to you in all those ways all at the same time all the time. We, as the imperfect recovering Iddicts we are (*Iddict* is my term for someone who is addicted to herself—her wants, her wisdom, her whims, her way.), usually lock on to either the righteousness/justice side of God or the compassion/love side of God.

To which side do you most often gravitate in your relationship with God?

Here's the deal with most of us Gomer Girls. We either gravitate toward the righteous/justice side of God and decide we are just plain unworthy and worthless—pond scum beyond the reach of grace. Or, we lean so hard into the compassion/love side of God that we think we are just fine, everything's good, sin isn't a big deal—beyond the need of grace.

Even though this is a big no no, I want you to compare yourself to someone else.

Where do you usually think you are on the continuum from "The Worst Pond Scum Ever" to "Practically Perfect in Every Way"? The Worst Pond Scum Ever means we feel we are totally beyond the reach of God's grace. Practically Perfect means that we feel we are beyond the need of God's grace.

On the Grace Scale below, place an "M" (that means you) on the spot which best represents where you are most of the time. Don't overthink it, just estimate.

1   2   3   4   5   6   7   8   9   10

WORST POND SCUM EVER   PRACTICALLY PERFECT

Now think of our girl Gomer. Place a "G" for Gomer on the spot which best represents where she was most of the time.

Now glance where you placed yourself and where you placed Gomer. Let me ask you some questions.

Do you find yourself moving back and forth on that scale based on your behavior?

What are some of the behaviors causing you to move back and forth on the continuum?

Do you think Gomer should have been nestled up right next to Practically Perfect when she was a chaste, faithful bride?

Do you think she should have been in the negatives, below pond scum, when she was committing adultery?

Was Gomer beyond the reach of grace?

Romans 3:23 says "all" have sinned. The "Practically Perfect" and Gomer alike. Their sins may be different, but their condition is the same—sinners who need grace. No one is beyond the need, or reach, of grace. Our behavior isn't what dictates where we land on the grace scale.

Israel got a little full of themselves in Hosea's day and thought they were good.

Read Hosea 5:5,11 and Hosea 7:10. Based on those verses, where do you think they would fall on the grace scale above? Why?

They were prideful and stumbling in their sin. They were determined to follow man's way, their own way. They were arrogant and unwilling to turn to God. When one behaves as they did, you may assume that they should be with the pond scum on the grace scale. You know, "we are so bad we are beyond reach of grace." But, the thing is, behavior doesn't determine where we place ourselves on that scale. Israel could have put themselves up there as "Practically Perfect" as far as not needing grace because they were prideful, arrogant, and thought they were good. After all, they worshiped Yahweh along with Baal. They were His chosen people ... blah, blah, blah.

The point is they were not so bad that God could not, or would not, reach them. No one can be so good that they do not need to be reached by God's grace.

I set you up with that scale. Anywhere you marked on that scale would not reflect your true condition. If you, Gomer, Israel, or I marked pond scum or Practically Perfect on the grace scale it reflects we are deceived.

> Find Hosea 10:13. What is the reason Israel was deceived? Hint: look at the last phrase.

Hosea said they had planted wickedness, reaped evil, and eaten the fruit of deception because they had depended on their own strength. When we depend on our own strength, the ultimate result is deception. We slip into Gomerisms and trust our wisdom that tells us we are beyond the need, or reach, of grace.

Here is your choice: Depend on grace or depend on self.

We were saved by grace. But until we live "saved" by grace we will never really experience the perfect, unfailing love of God—balanced in righteousness and love; justice, and compassion.

God has chosen to betroth Himself to you in righteousness forever; love, justice, and compassion are yours. Not because you earn or deserve them. You get them because God gives it. Grace.

> Which of those words mean the most to you and why? (*forever, righteousness, justice, love,* or *compassion*)

All of those words point in the same direction. They point to Jesus, "full of grace and truth."

Uh huh! And all the sisters said? Amen!

RESTING IN RESTORATION

You will call Me, "My husband,"
and no longer call Me, "My Baal."
HOSEA 2:16b, HCSB

We're finishing up this week and this chapter on a lovely high note. To review and get you back into context, read Hosea 2:14-23.

Everything you just read speaks to God's restoration of Israel and Hosea's restoration of Gomer. After reading those verses, how would you describe God?

What words come to mind?

For me, words like *Redeemer* and *Restorer* come to mind.

Now, I want you to read it again and try to glean from the verses what it is that God restored or is restoring and write it below. Don't be intimidated! If you're not used to doing Bible study this way, ask the Holy Spirit to guide you. He will. I know you can do it.

In verse 15: God is restoring ...

In verse 16: God is restoring ...

In verse 17: God is restoring ...

In verse 18: God is restoring ...

In verses 19,20: God restores ...

In verse 23: God restores ...

I'm not sure how you answered, but I love that you gave it a shot! Our answers may vary and that's OK. I will share with you my thoughts:

In verse 15: God is restoring security and safety, joy, and hope.

In verse 16: I think God is restoring position and dignity.

In verse 17: It seems God is restoring purity.

In verse 18: I see God restoring peace.

In verses 19,20: God restores a loving relationship.

Finally, in verse 23: I think God restores compassion and connection.

> Now, either look at your answers, or mine, and jot down what you most need God to restore in your life. Security? Joy? Hope? Loving relationship with Him? Dignity? Purity? Peace? Connection? Why?

God can restore what you lack and long for. He promised Judah and Israel He would restore them.

> What does Hosea 6:11 suggest to you?

Hosea was ministering to Israel, but, in this verse, He is addressing Judah. His words apply to Israel as well, and to me and to you too. You can see in Jeremiah 30:2-3 the same phrase about restoration applied to Israel.

> What did God say He would restore?

When you see the phrase about restoring their fortunes, you may think it means God will let His people win the lottery and get back all the money they lost when their local bank was robbed. That isn't what it means. It's better than that. That phrase is a Hebrew idiom which describes "being freed of any kind of circumstantial degradation or destruction." In other words, God will take away their indignity, shame, and humiliation.

That is how God restores you too. He not only gives back what the locusts have eaten, He restores you by preventing and removing indignity, shame, and humiliation.

Think about it. If you said you long for God to restore your sense of security, then as He removes your humiliation, your sense of security increases. Beautiful, huh?

God's people were like a priceless piece of silver that had forgotten its own worth and beauty. The ornate antique was tarnished and dented. It had been neglected, abused, and misused. Like a master silversmith, a restorer with a tender and skilled touch, God committed Himself to restoring them to the original beauty and glory for which they had been created. The restoration process includes cleaning, polishing, and repairing.

That means for us to experience God's restoration, we don't try to spray a pretty fragrance over what stinks in our lives, nor do we throw a bright white robe over the dirt that clings to us. Rather, to be restored, we receive correction if need be.

> The restoration process doesn't always feel good. In fact, what does Hosea 6:1-3 suggest to you about the process? Describe any aspects you see in the passage.

Hosea acknowledges that God has torn, but He will heal; He has broken, but He will bind up. Just like a furniture restorer sands and disassembles just to make the piece fit for restoration to its original state, God does the same. He did it for Israel and He does it for us. In the restoration process, humiliation and indignity are wiped away. Layers of shame are removed and more and more beauty is revealed. But just like a physical restoration, the process includes a lot of discomfort, some abrasion, and a willingess to submit to the hand of the craftsman.

Hosea removed Gomer's chains, set boundaries, and brought his wife home.

She was not only redeemed, but she was restored to her rightful position. Her shame and indignity were covered by his grace and acceptance. God wants to restore you in the same way.

Gomer Girl, can you rest in God's restoration? Will you let Him clean and repair, restoring you to your beauty and intended purpose?

If so, here is the response of Israel that you can echo.

It's at the end of Hosea's prophecy. Hosea 14 begins with a call to repentance and gives words to pray. The people of Israel needed to seek God's grace and forgiveness. They needed to denounce their self-reliance and dependence on Assyria.

> Their repentance was the beginning of their restoration. Read and meditate on Hosea 14 and pray those words to the Lord for your restoration also.

> Israel, return to Yahweh your God,
> for you have stumbled in your sin.
> Take words of repentance with you
> and return to the LORD.
> Say to Him: "Forgive all our sin
> and accept what is good,
> so that we may repay You
> with praise from our lips.
> Assyria will not save us,
> we will not ride on horses,
> and we will no longer proclaim, 'Our gods!'
> to the work of our hands.
> For the fatherless receives compassion in You."
> **HOSEA 14:1-3, HCSB**

Remember, it is His love that makes you lovely. By faith, choose to embrace your identity—the loved, accepted, complete beloved of God.

Malachi

We don't often hear much about Malachi, except in a tithing sermon (3:7-10) or to mention his book is the one right before the New Testament. Malachi has the last word in the Old Testament, and then is followed by a lot of silence.

As far as Malachi the person goes, we know very little. His name literally means "my messenger." We're not sure if "Malachi" was the prophet's job title or given name. What we do know is that as a prophet, he faithfully proclaimed God's message to His people. Included in the cast of characters we'll encounter in his prophecy are the Israelites and the temple priests.

The Book of Malachi was written around 460-430 B.C., the time of the second return of the exiled Jewish people under the leadership of Ezra. Malachi spoke to the hearts of a troubled people struggling with financial insecurity, religious skepticism, and personal disappointments.

The people of Judah had been indifferent to God, blaming their economic and social troubles on God's supposed unfaithfulness. They were treating one another faithlessly (especially their wives) and were profaning the temple by marrying pagan women. They were also withholding their tithes.

God commanded, and still commands, sincere worship with genuine faith and humility. This included honoring Him with pure offerings, being faithful to one another, and renewing the tithe of all they acquired to signify their recognition of the Lord as their God and King.

Malachi announced a coming day when the God of justice would come to judge the wicked and refine His people. He also spoke of hope. He pointed to God's demonstrations of love for His people, their unity with God and with one another, and a coming day of salvation and blessing for those who fear Him.

ABOUT MALACHI: A LOVE THAT NEVER LETS GO

Originally published in 2012, *Malachi: A Love that Never Lets Go* is an 8-session women's Bible study by Lisa Harper. In this study Lisa focuses on God's mercy. On our worst day, God doesn't walk away from us.

ABOUT LISA HARPER

A master storyteller, Lisa's writing and speaking connect the dots between the Bible era and modern life. A sought-after Bible teacher known for her authenticity, Lisa speaks at conferences around the world. When asked about her accomplishments Lisa said, "I'm so grateful for the opportunities God's given me, but don't forget, He often uses donkeys and rocks!" She notes her greatest accomplishment to date is getting to be Missy's mama. In April 2014, after a difficult two-year journey, Lisa finally got to bring her adopted daughter home from Haiti. And she hasn't stopped grinning since.

WEEK
5

God's Definitive
Declaration of Affection

I volunteer at a halfway house in downtown Nashville called "The Next Door" that's a faith-based, six-month residential program for women recovering from addiction to drugs or alcohol. If you've ever had the privilege of spending time with recovering addicts you know it's an amazing experience as well as a raggedly honest one. Women who've been busted and spent years in prison as a result don't usually feel the need to wear façades anymore. Frankly, I wish our congregations, small groups, and Sunday School classes were as authentic as my friends are who live in The Next Door house, because I think we're all addicts at heart.

In his book, *Addictions: A Banquet in the Grave*, academic and theologian Dr. Ed Welch wrote: "Addictions are ultimately a disorder of worship."[1] That means we're exhibiting addictive behavior anytime we don't have God squarely in our "soul hole" and so seek to satiate our need for love with anything—or anyone—else. I've never been dependant on drugs or alcohol but I've definitely been addicted to carbohydrates and abusive men.

Well anyway, as a result of volunteering at The Next Door, I've also started going to some Alcoholics Anonymous and Narcotics Anonymous meetings with my friends in recovery. I heard a story recently at one of those meetings that wedged itself deeply into my heart like a redemptive splinter. As is customary at every AA or NA meeting, a woman I'll call Shenequa (not her real name) began with the phrase, "Hi, my name is Shenequa, and I'm an alcoholic-addict." After the rest of the group responded with a hearty, "Hi, Shenequa," she exclaimed with a wide grin, "I was so thankful to be cleaning them tubs today, y'all!" As the rest of her story spilled out, I found out the day of the meeting coincided with her first day of employment at a downtown Nashville hotel.

Shenequa enthused about her new position as a full-time maid because she'd pounded the pavement for over a month and had turned in one hundred fourteen job applications before finally landing this gig. Mind you, it wasn't her first day of work but it was her first eight-hour shift with a company that pays Social Security taxes and gives its employees benefits. Her former job had been selling her body to men who sometimes handed her a $20 bill or a small rock of crack cocaine and often gave her a sexually transmitted disease or a closed fist across the face.

As I listened to Shenequa chatter about how grateful she is to work in a clean, air-conditioned environment with nice people, I found myself wondering how many "tricks" she forced herself to perform to feed her eight young children before committing herself to recovery. How many times she closed her eyes and peeled off her clothes in a desperate attempt to get just one more hit of a narcotic powerful enough to numb her heart and mind to the harsh realities of her life for a few hours.

I can't imagine the torture of dragging myself out of bed every day and trudging through a life that difficult with so little light at the end of the tunnel. Yet not only did Shenequa drag herself out of bed, by the grace of a God she'd heard about as a child and never stopped believing in, she ultimately dragged herself to a treatment center and admitted she needed help defeating the beast of drug addiction.

I don't think I'll ever forget the last thing Shenequa said at that meeting. She explained how she'd stood up to stretch in the hotel bathroom she was cleaning and caught her reflection in the mirror. Her voice caught for a second as she was describing the scene and she took a deep breath to steady herself, then she said softly, "That's the first time since I was a little girl that I looked in the mirror and liked what I seen." Shenequa is beginning to remember who God created her to be. She's beginning to believe again how much her heavenly Father adores her.

Malachi's peers were polar opposites of Shenequa. Instead of remembering they were God's children whom He had always protected and provided for, they were allowing their present-day circumstances to fog up the mirror reflecting their heavenly Father's faithfulness. They'd allowed their entire history as recipients of God's lavish mercy to become clouded over. Instead of looking in the glass and smiling in recognition that they bore their divine Dad's image, they focused in on a smudge at the edge and the mildew on the shower curtain behind them. They'd all but forgotten how their value, hope, peace, and future were linked to God's love. So their Creator Redeemer clears His throat, cups His hands around His mouth, and reminds them.

A phrase like "their Creator Redeemer clears His throat, cups His hands around His mouth, and reminds them" is an anthropomorphism, which means attributing human characteristics or behavior to nonhuman things like God or cartoon animals. Anthropomorphisms are often found in biblical imagery, such as when David talks about the heavens being the work of God's "fingers" in Psalm 8:3 to emphasize how even the magnitude of creation is dwarfed by the majesty of our divine King.

God's love is immutable
Only God is perfectly faithful.
A love that never lets go.   He has loved many tumblers.

II Samuel 4:4 , 1 Samuel 20:15
2 Samuel 9 (20 yrs later) : 2-5 , 7, 13

Definitive declaration of God's redeeming love.

OUTLINE

SCENE 1 assertion (from God): Malachi 1:2a

SCENE 2 questioning (from Israel): Malachi 1:2b

SCENE 3 response (from God): Malachi 1:2c-3

SCENE 4 implication (to Israel): Malachi 1:4-5

SETTING THE STAGE

Yesterday I went for a long trail run in the beautiful Natchez Trace wilderness near where I live in the boondocks south of Nashville. I began my workout with a smile and a happy heart, absolutely smitten by the colors of fall in the canopy of leaves overhead. But halfway up the first big hill, my body began to boycott.

My lower back huffed, "I'm tired of supporting Lisa while she pretends to be a mountain goat; I'm too old for this and have decided to resign." My ankles indignantly replied, "You don't have anything to whine about you big baby, we're the ones stuck down here next to rocks, logs, and horse manure—if she scrapes us again, we're going to pay her back with a nasty sprain." My inner thighs immediately yelled, "Shut up down there! We've got an emergency situation up here. If she runs any faster the friction between us is bound to set this forest on fire!"

My body is in a transitional phase. Swiftly approaching fifty, this jar of clay is transitioning from loose to stiff, from resilient to brittle, from perky to saggy. The good news is these physical shifts provide tangible reminders that the earthly existence our Creator allows us is in a constant state of change. I'm learning that the harder we resist change, the harder reality feels when we collide into it headfirst! Change is inevitable, but trusting God through it is a choice. The Israelites were in a massive transitional phase during the season Malachi prophesied.

They'd moved from captivity in Babylon back to a degree of independence in Israel; from a secure—albeit confined—existence to risky freedom pockmarked with uncertainty about where they'd live, how they'd put food on the table, and what they should do to protect themselves from their enemies.

What is the biggest transition you're going through right now? Do you feel like you're moving from captivity to freedom, or does your transition seem to be leading you to a more confining place?

The temple their grandparents reminisced about during those long decades in captivity had been demolished. Now standing in its place atop a high hill in Jerusalem was a much smaller church with warped vinyl siding, secondhand furniture, and no big screens for PowerPoint® (see Ezra 3:12).

> Does a spiritual "mountaintop" experience in your past cause you to feel nostalgic? If so, do you think it ever keeps you from fully engaging in what God is currently doing in your life?

They no longer had the privilege of joyfully serving under a great, divinely chosen king like David and instead had to submit to the authority of a mundane civil ruler (see Mal. 1:8).

> Who are some of your favorite former "spiritual leaders" (for example: pastors, Sunday School teachers, or camp counselors from your childhood or adolescence)? Why did they have such a positive impact on you?

Their formerly safe neighborhoods, once filled with the familiar faces of extended family and friends, had morphed into strange, multinational melting pots. Main Street was now dotted with ethnic restaurants. Falafels and pomegranate juice were swiftly being replaced by oblong sandwiches called burr-eetoes and fizzy brown drinks called soe-duhs. Much to their parent's chagrin, some of their cousins had even married foreigners who talked funny (see Mal. 2:11). Since they didn't like the changes that had come their way, God's people decided to stage a boycott.

Instead of trusting their heavenly Father—who had always provided for them and protected them—they sat down with a collective *harrumph*, poked out their bottom lips, and began to seriously doubt His goodness.

> Can you personally relate to how the Israelites seem to be somewhat stuck in their past and dissatisfied with their present? If so, in what specific ways can you relate?

INTRODUCING NEW CHARACTERS

We've already met Malachi and his peers, and the Creator Redeemer of the Universe certainly needs no introduction, so the only character left to account for in this disputation is that scaly, scorched-breath, divine antagonist named Lucifer (see Isa. 14:12), also known as "Satan" (Job 1:5-7); the devil (see Matt. 4:1-3); the "dragon" (Rev. 12); the deceiver (see John 8:42-44); and the "serpent" or snake (Gen. 3). He's been spewing treachery and deceit since his whopping ego became too heavy for his angelic wings to tote around and he tumbled from God's glorious presence with a resounding splat (see Isa. 14:12-18; Ezekiel 28:12-18; Luke 10:18).

Satan not only lost his ability to fly, he lost his job directing the choir in heaven and became the chief rival of his former Boss, the Holy Trinity. Since his humiliating plummet from grace, Satan now spends most of his time slinking around here on earth, whispering insidious things into the ears of God's most overwhelmed and exhausted image-bearers.

> How has Lucifer tried to lure you away from the promise of God's love lately? (See John 8:42-44.)

The deceiver has been trying to convince humanity that God didn't—or couldn't—love them since the beginning of time. Remember the hateful stunt he pulled on our great-great and then some grandmother Eve? Here she was completely flabbergasted about being the first female in the universe—I can't begin to imagine the pressure coming with that distinction—and was surely a bit blinded by the sights and sounds of Eden, when the old snake slithered up next to her and said coyly, "You know Eva-licious, if God really loved you, He would let you eat the fruit from any tree in the garden. I mean you are burning the candle at both ends, what with alphabetizing all those names Adam came up with for every creature plus having to carry around all the heavy stuff until the stitches heal from his rib-removal surgery. So I think you deserve to eat whatever you want. If I was your daddy, I wouldn't put any restrictions on you!"

Ugh, makes you want to rip that forked tongue right out of his mouth, doesn't it? Unfortunately, in Malachi's day the nation of Israel was in such a state of disappointment and despair regarding the changes they faced on returning home from Babylon that they stopped standing guard against the lizard bent on their destruction. Soon enough the lies he was whispering about God's lack of affection and concern for them began to sound uncannily like the truth. Let's look at the first disputation.

Israel is the only nation ever specifically chosen by God for a covenantal relationship. The Old Testament historical books—Joshua, Judges, Ruth, 1 Samuel, 2 Samuel, 1 Kings, 2 Kings, 1 Chronicles, 2 Chronicles, Ezra, Nehemiah, and Esther—reveal how God established Israel as His very own people group and how He chose the Israelites to be His ambassadors to other nations.

SCENE ONE

ASSERTION (FROM GOD):

"I have loved you," says the LORD.
MALACHI 1:2a, ESV

In rhetorical disputation what God says first typically sets the tone and creates the "flavor" for the whole passage. This means the first prophetic meal served in Malachi began with dessert because it just doesn't get any sweeter than the Creator of the Universe saying I. Have. Loved. You.

The tense of the Hebrew verb in Malachi 1:2a could be translated with the phrase, "'I love you,' Yahweh said."[2] In this simple statement, God clarifies that He has already fulfilled the deepest desire of every human heart to be fully known, completely accepted, and unconditionally adored. God wasn't holding up a carrot trying to tempt the Israelites back toward faithfulness. He's not saying, "If y'all straighten up and behave like I told you, then I'll think about loving you." There's no condition to God's pronouncement of enduring affection. It's not a wobbly, if-the-planets-align-I'll-do-it, kind of pledge. It's a statement of historical fact. The Creator of the Universe had loved His chosen people, the Israelites, throughout every single moment of their lives.

How does your head react to the fact that God loves you?

How about your heart? What emotional response does the fact of God's affection for you prompt?

I think the way our heavenly Father communicates His compassion without guile is the bomb! I'm so glad God isn't a coy suitor. He doesn't act like a seventh-grade boy at the movies with us who jams his hands in his pockets in an attempt to look cool. Thank goodness the Lover of our soul has instead always been publicly passionate about His people. Remember how He advertised His relationship with the Israelites in the wilderness? How He hovered over them like a cloud by day and a pillar of fire at night (see Ex. 13:17-22)? That's like a supernatural blimp of commitment—God's overt declarations of affection make Barry White sound like a lisping schoolboy. Anybody blushing yet?

Read Song of Songs 2:4; 4:9. What's the most overt romantic gesture someone's ever done for you? How did you react to their overture?

Humanly speaking, whose affection (romantic, platonic, or familial) can you trust in the most? When you look back over the course of your life, has someone always seemed to love you? If so, who is that person (or people) and why do you think their love for you is so consistent?

When have you felt the most secure in God's everlasting love for you? (See Ps. 136:2; Rom. 8:35-39.)

On a scale of 1 to 10, with 1 being absolute disbelief and 10 being absolute security, how confident are you regarding God's affection for you today?

| 1 | 2 | 3 | 4 | 5 | 6 | 7 | 8 | 9 | 10 |

absolute disbelief   absolute security

SCENE TWO

QUESTIONING (FROM ISRAEL):

"How have you loved us?"
MALACHI 1:2b, ESV

In spite of God's ardency, Malachi's buddies arched their eyebrows in doubt over His assertion. After a slow, sweeping look at the poverty and chaos surrounding them, they let out a long sigh and asked, "How have you loved us?"

The first time I studied the Book of Malachi and read their cheeky inquiry, I was tempted to retort, "Really, y'all? I mean, come on! Yahweh rescued you from Egypt, He dried up an entire ocean so you wouldn't get your tootsies wet on your trek to freedom, He showered you with Twinkies® in the wilderness, and He gave you first dibs on national holidays—come on! How about a little less whining here, people? How about showing some gratitude instead of calling God's fidelity into question?"

When I silenced the peanut gallery in my head and really pondered the starkness of the Israelite's postexilic circumstances—how they'd attended one too many funerals of their friends and family members, how their national dignity had been dragged through the mud, how they'd been forced to drain their savings accounts and rack up huge debt just to eek out a living, and how they lugged boxes of their meager possessions downstairs to their mother-in-law's tiny basement to have someplace indoors for their kids to sleep—I stopped judging and started empathizing.

Because I know what it's like to become so distracted by my own disappointment, so preoccupied with my own pain, that I glance right past God's grace. I'm not minimizing the fact that the Israelites doubted God's mercy, but I can totally relate to it. I'm guilty of wasting big chunks on the calendar of my life living like an emotional agnostic too. How about you?

Compare God's covenant promises to Abraham (founding father of the Israelite nation) with what actually occurred prior to Malachi's era by reading Genesis 12:1-3; 2 Chronicles 36:15-23.

In light of their recent history, how much hope do you think the Israelites held out that God would actually come through on what He had promised Abraham?

What "hope deferred" (an unfulfilled dream or promise, Prov. 13:12) made you the most heartsick in the past?

With what unfulfilled dream are you currently dealing?

Has your disappointment made you move toward God or away from Him? Why do you think it has that effect?

A holy song is a wonderful illustration of how God allows His people to wrestle honestly with disappointment. The psalms were originally crafted as the hymn book of the Old Testament.[3] Read Psalm 42 and ask yourself how would you relate this divine blues tune to the seasons of your life thus far?

How would you relate in the beginning (vv. 1-4)?

How would you relate in the middle (vv. 5-7)?

How would you relate in the end (vv. 8-11)?

SCENE THREE

RESPONSE (FROM GOD):

"Is not Esau Jacob's brother?" declares the LORD. "Yet I have loved Jacob but Esau I have hated. I have laid waste his hill country and left his heritage to jackals of the desert."
MALACHI 1:2c-3, ESV

God's response here seems odd if not completely disconnected, as if He got distracted by a football game playing on the television behind Israel's head and forgot what they were talking about for a moment. But of course, that can't be the case because our Creator is perfectly omniscient and never misses a beat. God has simply switched gears in their conversation to jar the Israelites into considering the historicity of His faithfulness.

I can totally picture them leaning forward when God asked the rhetorical question: "Is not Esau Jacob's brother?" Because they realized immediately that He was referring to a colorful story about two brothers—fraternal twins actually—named Jacob and Esau who got themselves into the messiest food fight of all times. The Israelites were familiar with this tale because it had been told and retold among them for generations.

The story began with Abraham and Isaac. When Isaac was forty years old he married Rebekah, but they had no children. Isaac prayed for Rebekah, and God answered his prayer. Rebekah became pregnant, but it was a troubled pregnancy with twins who fought in her womb. She went to God to ask about the struggle within her, and God told her she was bearing two nations. The boys born to her would sire two countries and the older would serve the younger.

In the ancient Near Eastern language of Malachi, the antonyms *love* and *hate* are not indicative of petty human emotion.[4] In fact, the biblical idiom "to hate" usually means to love someone or something less rather than to have extreme animosity for someone or something (see Gen. 29:30-33; 1 Sam. 1:2-5; Matt. 10:37; Luke 14:25-26).

Isaac was sixty years old when the boys were born. The first was reddish and hairy; they named him Esau meaning Hairy. The other brother was born with his fist clutched tight to Esau's heel; they named him Jacob, meaning Heel.

When the boys grew up, Esau became an outdoorsman and a hunter. Jacob became a quiet man preferring life indoors. Isaac loved Esau because he loved to eat the game Esau brought home, but Rebekah loved Jacob.

One day Jacob was cooking a stew. Esau came in from the field, starved. Esau said to Jacob, "Give me some of that red stew—I'm starved!" That's how he came to be called Edom (Red). Jacob said, "Make me a trade: my stew for your rights as the firstborn." Esau said, "I'm starving! What good is a birthright if I'm dead?" Jacob said, "First, swear to me." And he did it. On oath Esau traded away his rights as the firstborn.

> Jacob gave him bread and the stew of lentils. He ate and drank, got up and left. That's how Esau shrugged off his rights as the firstborn.
> GENESIS 25:29-34, The Message

The kicker of this true tale is that Hairy's (Esau) offspring grew up and formed the nation of Edom, while Heely's (Jacob) offspring went on to become the nation of Israel. God chose Jacob—the younger twin—to be the specific grandson of Abraham through whom His covenant people, the Jews, would come. Sadly, all of Esau's kids and grandkids and great-grandkids were sentenced to live their lives outside the circle of God's sovereign favor. Ultimately, as a result of their continued rebellion against God, all the inhabitants of Edom were completely destroyed.

My guess is the Israelites' eyes got really round after this response from God because His words were a thunderous reminder of their status as class favorites.

> Reread Genesis 25:19-34 in your Bible. With which of the twins do you identify most? Why?

> Do you think it's "fair" that God favored Jacob over Esau? Explain.

How does the story of Jacob and Esau shed light on Paul's sermon in Ephesians 2 about our salvation being a free gift from God that isn't based on our morality or lack thereof?

Isaiah chapters 34–35 describes the future for the descendants of Jacob and Esau. Chapter 34 pictures the future for Edom (see Isa. 34:9-10). Chapter 35 focuses on Israel's future from Isaiah's perspective.

If you were writing a book or a screenplay about either of those chapters, what title would you give each?

Edom's future:

Israel's future:

Which verse from Isaiah 35 would you choose as a theme verse for your and/or your family's future?

How would you paraphrase that theme verse into language that a child could understand?

Read Matthew 10:37; Luke 14:25-27. Who have you had to love less to get closer to Jesus?

DAY 5

SCENE FOUR

IMPLICATION (TO ISRAEL):

"Your own eyes shall see this."
MALACHI 1:5, ESV

Those of us who speak or sing at Christian women's conferences get pretty punchy when we have to sit on a side stage for about several hours on a weekend. I honestly think my bottom has gotten flatter and wider over the past few years as a result! However, since the cameras sometimes pan in our direction thereby projecting us on giant screens for all the attendees to see, we're expected to behave. But sometimes we just can't help ourselves.

Such was the case recently when seconds before Sheila Walsh walked on stage I bet her she couldn't weave the word *raccoon* into her talk. Someone had told a story about raccoons raiding their trash cans on our break so it was the first unsuitable word that came to my mind.

Brave Scottish lass that she is, Sheila wasn't even rattled by my last-second dare. Instead she grinned at me triumphantly and said, "Done!" before waltzing onstage. I don't remember exactly how she wove raccoon into her expositional message from the New Testament, but I do remember it was seamless.

The implication here in verse 5 is the divine version of "Done!" It's a definitive promise from the Creator and Sustainer of the Universe that the Israelites will see the permanent demise of their archenemy, the Edomites. Yet in spite of their galvanizing history lesson only moments before, I think Malachi's peers now furrowed their eyebrows and crossed their arms dubiously. Because from their finite human perspective, Edom was still flourishing and they were still floundering. It was as if God had prematurely presented the Oscar to a clumsy ingénue who'd forgotten her lines and fallen off the stage while Meryl Streep was waiting in the wings dressed in Armani couture. His "done" just didn't seem plausible given their current circumstances.

The little Book of Obadiah speaks to the nation of Edom. "Though you soar aloft like the eagle, though your nest is set among the stars, from there I will bring you down, declares the LORD" (Obad. 4, ESV).

Do you know someone who's currently flying high like an eagle in spite of the fact that they're deceitful, abusive, and/or extremely self-centered? If so, how do you feel about the fact that they seem to be benefitting from hurting others—perhaps even you?

In Psalm 69 David poured out his heart in a time of great distress. Read Psalm 69:16-29 and describe the season in your life when you could most identify with some of David's complaints in this sad song.

Do you typically consider God slow when it comes to judging the wicked people who are polluting your little corner of the world or just right with regard to how and when He doles out consequences to the wicked?

Psalm 139:19-24 makes some rather radical statements about hating the enemies of God. How would you describe the healthy tension between having a strong heart that rears up against evil and having a soft heart that submits to the authority of the Holy Spirit?

Imagine you are teaching Sabbath school in Malachi's time. How would you explain Romans 5:1-5 to the Israelites?

MINING PERSONAL JEWELS FROM MALACHI'S STORY

Write Romans 5:1-5 as nicely and neatly as you can on an index card or sheet of paper with your nondominant hand. If you're right-handed, use your left hand and vice versa; if you're ambidextrous, this is going to be a piece of cake! While you're writing out all five verses, pray for God to help you appreciate things that take a long time. Then when you finish, post your artwork in a public place like your refrigerator at home or your computer monitor at the office to practice appreciating something that took a relatively long time to create and didn't come out perfectly!

LEARNING TO HOPE

1. Create a top 10 waiting list of things you've almost stopped hoping for.

2. Pray through your list, asking God to breathe life into the hopes and dreams that are in alignment with His will for your life and to give you wisdom regarding what hopes and dreams to let go of.

3. Consider sharing your waiting list with a few other Christian girlfriends in order to have support in this journey toward really taking God at His word!

ENDNOTES

GIDEON

1. Jeff Lucas, *Gideon: Power from Weakness* (Franklin, TN: Authentic Publishers, 2004), 91

NEHEMIAH

1. David Kidner, *Tyndale Old Testament Commentaries, vol. 12, Ezra and Nehemiah* (Downers Grove, IL: InterVarsity Press, 1979) 89.
2. Mervin Breneman, *The New American Commentary, vol. 10, Ezra, Nehemiah, Esther* (Nashville, TN: Broadman & Holman Publishers, 1993), 182–84.
3. David J.A. Clines, as quoted by Breneman, *The New American Commentary, vol. 10, Ezra, Nehemiah, Esther* (Nashville, TN: Broadman & Holman Publishers, 1993) 189.
4. Angie Smith, *I Will Carry You* (Nashville, TN: B&H Publishing Group, 2010), 158.
5. H. G. M. Williamson, *Word Biblical Commentary, vol. 16, Ezra Nehemiah* (Nashville, TN: Thomas Nelson, 1985), 212.
6. Breneman, *The New American Commentary*, 193.
7. Williamson, *Word Biblical Commentary*, 226.

ESTHER

1. Karen H. Jobes, "Esther" in *The NIV Application Commentary* (Grand Rapids, MI: Zondervan, 1999), 138.
2. N. T. Wright. *Following Jesus* (Grand Rapids, MI: William B. Eerdsman Publishing Company, 1988), 66-68.
3. A. Boyd Luter & Barry C. Davis. *God Behind the Seen* (Grand Rapids, MI: Baker Book House, 1995), 217.
4. Leslie C. Allen and Timothy S. Laniak. "Ezra, Nehemiah, Esther" in the *New International Biblical Commentary* (Peabody, MA: Hendrickson Publishers, Inc., 2003), 92,94-95.
5. Todd McCarthy. "Film Reviews Through the Years," *Variety* [online], 20 November 1993 [cited 4 February 2008]. Available from the Internet: www.variety.com/index. asp?layout=variety100&reviewid=VE11117487981&content=jump&jump=review&category=1935&cs=1.
6. Jobes, 132.
7. J. G. McConville. *Ezra, Nehemiah, and Esther* (Louisville, KY: Westminster John Knox Press, 1985), 171.
8. David J. A. Clines. *The Esther Scroll* (Sheffield, England: JSOT Press, 1984), 36.
9. Jobes, 137.
10. Mervin Breneman. *The New American Commentary: Ezra, Nehemiah, and Esther* (Nashville: Broadman Press, 1993), 337.

HOSEA

1. C. S. Lewis, *The Great Divorce* (New York, NY: Harper Collins, 1973), 69.

MALACHI

1. Edward T. Welch, *Addictions: A Banquet in the Grave* (Phillipsburg, NJ: P&R Publishing, 2001), xvi.
2. Thomas Edward McComiskey, ed., *The Minor Prophets: An Exegetical and Expository Commentary* (Grand Rapids, MI: Baker Academic, 1992), 1281.
3. Tremper Longman III, *How to Read the Psalms* (Downers Grove, IL: InterVarsity, 1988), 24.
4. McComiskey, 1283–84.

LEADER GUIDE

First, we want to say how thankful we are for you, the leader. Thank you for your willingness to dive into Scripture, brew the coffee, place the chairs, and set aside the time regularly to meet with other women. We're grateful for you and praying for you as you lead this study.

This study is a bit unusual for us. We've tried to anticipate your questions in the introduction and here in the leader guide. We want you to use this study however it works best for you and your group. If you want to follow this leader guide to the letter, do that! If you want to do your own thing, feel free! We want to give you all the tools you might need, but we are certain God has ordained your time with your specific group in your specific setting.

Here are a few tips to help you as you prepare.

1. VIDEO TEACHING. The videos for this study are available in the leader kit (item number 005809761) as well as by download (you can rent or buy the digital videos) at LifeWay.com/TheFaithful. We strongly recommend you use the teaching videos as a part of this study, but you can still discover truth from Scripture and grow in your walk with God simply doing the print portion if your setting doesn't allow for video.

2. GET THE WORD OUT. Be sure to advertise the study early and utilize all methods for getting the word out. Post it on your church's website, send emails to potential attendees, and promote it on all forms of social media. It's best to start advertising the study four to six weeks before it begins. The study is five sessions long, which means you will meet five times. There are also options to meet a sixth and seventh time if you'd like to have an introductory week to get to know one another and a closing/review week at the end. Visit LifeWay.com/TheFaithful for free promotional materials to help get the word out about your study.

3. SCHEDULE. This study is different in that the video lengths vary greatly from session to session. We recommend allowing an hour and a half for each session, providing time for discussion after the longest video (Session 3). You could also divide some video sessions into two weeks if that works best for your group. Be sure to make everyone aware of the schedule ahead of time and start promptly each week to honor everyone's time. In your group time, you will view the video teaching together and discuss what you're learning. Close with a time of prayer.

4. STAY IN TOUCH. Prepare a sign up sheet with space for names, email addresses, and phone numbers. You may also include information like

birthdays, social media handles, and favorite candy so that you can foster community among group members.

5. GET COZY. Make an effort to create a comfortable environment for group meetings. Arrange chairs in a circle to encourage conversation. If your group is large, you may want to watch the video teaching together and then split into smaller groups for the discussion time. If you choose to do so, enlist discussion leaders for each group to keep the conversation moving and focused.

6. CHILDCARE. Be sure to check with participants to see if childcare is needed and organize leaders and space for the children in advance.

7. BIBLE STUDY BOOKS. Each participant will need a Bible study book. Make sure you leave plenty of time for all the books to be ordered and received between announcing and starting your Bible study. Consider offering a scholarship or buy-one-give-one option for those who cannot afford a study book on their own.

8. EARLY PREP. Because this study is a little different than many of our studies, we strongly suggest reading through all of the leader guide before the first session. You may want to think through the different ways this study can be conducted and how it will work best for your group. Make sure you secure a DVD player and TV or whatever equipment you may need to watch the videos. If you don't already know, learn how to work the tech equipment needed or line up assistance to help in that area. We recommed watching the video sessions previous to your meeting, taking note of anything you may want to highlight from the teaching. Look over the discussion questions, as well, so that you are prepared to lead the conversation.

9. PERSONAL STUDY. Between each meeting, there are five days of personal study to complete in the Bible study book. Each of these varies in length due to the different authors for each week's study.

10. PRAYER. Most importantly, be sure to pray for the women who attend the study. And pray for yourself as you prepare to lead. Ask God to draw the women closer to Him and teach them to be faithful to Him as He continues to show faithfulness to each of you.

We've provided a leader guide for each session. Remember these are simply suggestions for how to use your time together. We want to empower you as you lead to do what is best for your group!

OPTIONAL INTRODUCTORY SESSION

This video session is 02:34 long.

1. Welcome women to the study and distribute Bible study books.

2. Make introductions, asking women what drew them to this Bible study.

3. Watch the Introduction video.

4. Following the video, lead women in discussion, using the following prompts:

   • How would you define the word *faith*? What does it mean to be faithful?

   • Is there someone in your life who has been faithful to you? to God? How did they demonstrate that faithfulness?

   • When has it been easy for you to be faithful? When has it been difficult?

   • How can we pray for one another this week?

5. Close the session with prayer.

SESSION 1 - GIDEON

This video session is 43:32 long.

1. If you chose not to have the optional Introductory Session, make introductions and watch the Introductory Session video.

2. Introduce Gideon. Ask who is familiar with his life and story in the Bible.

3. Watch the Session 1 video teaching on Gideon.

4. Following the video, lead women in discussion, using the following prompts:

   • What stood out to you about the video teaching?

   • In what ways have you had to "deal with the Midianites" in your life?

   • How can we know what is true of us? Are there any verses in Scripture you return to in order to remind yourself what is true? Share those with the group.

5. Share prayer requests and pray as a group before you leave.

SESSION 2 - NEHEMIAH

This video session is 23:04 long.

1. Welcome everyone and ask what they learned studying Gideon this week. Use the following questions to review the personal study from the week:

   - God used Gideon's everyday task of threshing in his calling. How do you see God possibly using one or more of your daily tasks in the calling He has for your life?

   - What do your routine tasks say to you about God's faithfulness?

   - What would receiving, believing, and walking in what God says about you do in your life? What would change about the next 24 hours if you believed what God said?

2. Introduce Nehemiah. Ask what people know about his life and story.

3. Watch the Session 2 video teaching on Nehemiah.

4. Following the video, lead the group in discussion, asking the following questions:

   - How has today's teaching caused you to think differently about repentence (see Neh. 1:6-7)?

   - In what ways does personal repentance free you from constantly focusing on the sin and shortcomings of others?

   - How did Katie's story impact the way you think about repentance? What impacted you the most?

   - Brainstorm ways you can get outside your comfort zone and serve others both here and around the world. Maybe there is even a project you could complete as a group to serve your neighbors!

5. Close in prayer.

SESSION 3 - ESTHER

This video is 1:05:32 long.

1. Welcome everyone and ask what they learned this week studying Nehemiah. Use the following queastions to promote conversation:

   - What's one of the greatest areas of need you see in your church or community? How were you challenged or helped by the way Nehemiah assessed the needs in Jerusalem?

   - What unforgettable memories do you have of serving God with others?

   - What are you "rebuilding" in your life right now? What makes rebuilding sometimes more difficult than building?

2. Introduce Esther. Discuss what you know about her and her story.

3. Watch the Session 3 video on Esther.

4. Following the video, lead the group in discussion, asking the following questions:

   - What stood out to you in the video teaching?

   - If anyone feels comfortable, invite them to share their "If _____, then God" statements with the group.

   - How have you seen others you know to take the courage and stand boldly "for such a time as this"?

5. Close your group in prayer.

SESSION 4 - HOSEA

This video session is 32:07 long.

1. Welcome the group and ask about studying Esther. Discuss questions that may have come up during the personal study. Review the previous week's study with the following questions:

   - Has God ever allowed threat of trouble in your life to drive you to your knees? If so, what did you learn from the experience?

- What recent inconveniences have you been tempted to treat like true tribulations?

- Think of another way we can try to help someone in crisis by, figuratively speaking, handing him or her something else to put on.

2. Introduce Hosea. What does the group know about Hosea's story?

3. Watch the Session 4 video on Hosea.

4. Following the video, lead the group in discussion, asking the following questions:

- What stood out to you in the video teaching?

- What did you learn about what it means to know God?

- Have you ever been guilty of sacrificing relationship with God for activity for Him? What did that look like for you?

- How can you begin to know God more deeply this week?

5. Close in prayer.

SESSION 5 - MALACHI

This video session is 27:40 long.

1. Welcome the group and ask what they learned this week about Hosea's story. Discuss the previous week's study using the following questions:

- How difficult do you find it to internalize the value 1 Peter 1:18-19 places on you?

- Which of the following words mean the most to you and why: *forever, righteousness, justice,* or *compassion*?

- How do you relate to the discussion of God restoring us? What has He restored for you, or what do you desire for Him to restore?

2. Introduce Malachi. Is anyone in your group familiar with this prophet?

3. Watch the Session 5 video on Malachi.

4. Following the video, lead the group in discussion, asking the following questions:

- When did you first realize God loves girls who limp?

- How have you sensed God's affection while limping?

- What does this last video teach us about God's faithfulness?

5. Close in prayer.

OPTIONAL WRAP-UP SESSION

If you would like to get together one last time to review the personal study on Malachi, feel free to use the following questions as a guide. Consider sharing a meal for this last meeting as a way to celebrate God's faithfulness to your group over the last several weeks.

- What is the biggest transition you're going through right now? Do you feel like you're moving from captivity to freedom, or does your transformation seem to be leading you to a more confining place?

- How does your head react to the fact that God loves you? How about your heart? What emotional response does the fact of God's affection for you prompt?

- Has your disappointment in life made you move toward God or away from Him? Why do you think it has that effect?

- What are ways this group can continue to encourage and pray for you in the coming weeks and months?

Conclude this final session in prayer. Share any upcoming ministry and Bible study events group members might like to participate in.

APPENDIX 1
CONTINUE IN BIBLE STUDY

Perhaps you want to learn more about the heroes in the Old Testament or you simply desire to dive into studying God's Word for yourself.

Bible studies like this one will help you connect with other believers who are learning from God's Word. They provide you with a specific time and place to focus on an aspect or book of the Bible and how it applies to your life now. However, nothing compares to a daily personal encounter with God.

We study the Bible to:

- Know the truth. We want to think clearly about what God says is true and valuable (see 2 Pet. 1:20-21).

- Know God in a personal relationship (see 1 Cor. 1:21; Gal. 4:8-9; 1 Tim. 4:16).

- Live well for God in this world. Living out His will expresses our love for Him (see John 14:23-24; Rom. 12:2; 1 Thess. 4:1-8; 2 Tim. 3:16-17).

- Experience God's freedom, grace, peace, hope, and joy (see Ps. 119:111; John 8:32; Rom. 15:4; 2 Pet. 1:2).

- Grow spiritually as we reject conformity to the world and are changed by the renewing of our minds (see Rom 12:2; 1 Pet. 2:1-2).

- Minister to other Christ followers and to those who have yet to respond to the gospel (see Josh. 1:8; 2 Tim. 2:15; 3:16-17; Eph. 6:11-17; 2 Pet. 2:1-2).

- Guard ourselves from sin and error (see Eph. 6:11-17; 2 Pet. 2:1-2).

- Build up as a Christian community with others in the body of Christ (see Acts 20:32; Eph. 4:14-16).[1]

If you do not already have a daily habit of spending time with God reading His Word, commit to selecting a time and place. Choose the time of day that works best for you and make it a priority. Keep your Bible and study materials in your meeting place. Develop a balanced plan for Bible reading or find one online. Make notes to see how God is speaking, and respond to Him in prayer. Strive for consistency as your main goal.[2]

1. George H. Guthrie, *Read the Bible for Life* (Nashville, TN: LifeWay Press, 2010), 16.
2. Ibid., 18.

APPENDIX 2
START A BIBLE STUDY TOOLBOX

As you can, begin to build a Bible study toolbox of resources to enhance your understanding of the Bible. A good study Bible in an understandable translation is essential. In choosing a Bible translation, look for one that uses the most reliable Hebrew and Greek manuscripts while being readable.

Here are a few other tools you may find helpful to add to your Bible study toolbox.

BIBLE ATLAS - Maps, charts, and photographs that illustrate the land, sites, and concepts in the Bible.

BIBLE DICTIONARY - Alphabetical list of key terms, places, people, events, and concepts in the Bible.

BIBLE ENCYCLOPEDIA - Articles about people, events, and places in the Bible, including history, religious environment, culture, language, and literature, as well as cross-references of other Scripture verses.

BIBLE COMMENTARY - Detailed theological analysis of specific verses and passages of Scripture. Includes a background introductory section for each book of the Bible, followed by detailed commentary of Scripture verse by verse.

BIBLE CONCORDANCE - Alphabetical index of important words in Scripture and the references of texts in which they are found.

ONLINE RESOURCES - Wordsearch Bible offers many of these resources free of charge with their digital library.

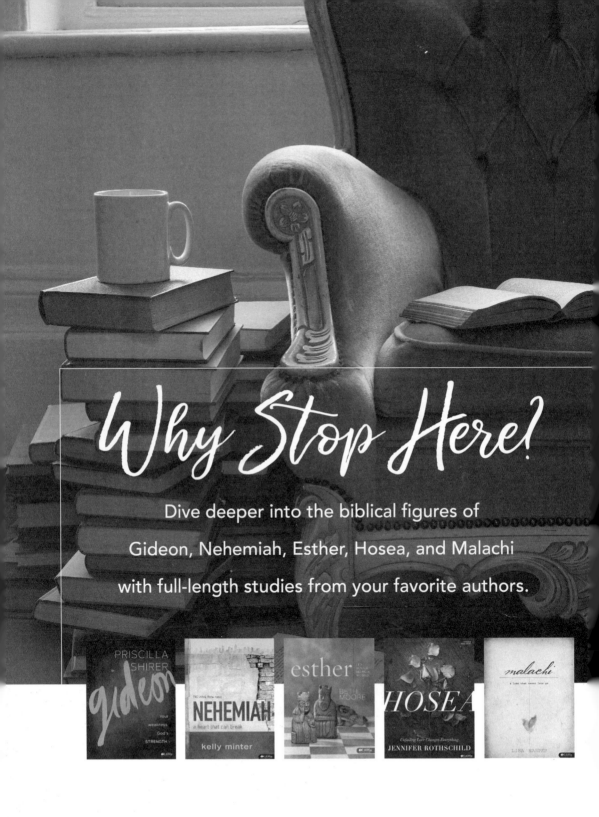